Series Editor

PAOLO BERTINETTI

Professor of English Literature,
University of Turin

Selection, introduction, notes and activities
© 1998 Cideb Editrice, Genoa

Edited by Elvira Poggi Repetto, Rebecca Raynes

First edition: September 1998

10 9 8 7 6 5 4 3 2 1

The author would like to thank Linda Rosenberg for her help with
Yiddish terms.

The publisher would like to thank the following for permission to
reproduce copyright material.

© A. P. Watt Ltd on behalf of Nadine Gordimer for 'The Bridegroom'.
© Heinemann for 'Minutes of Glory' by Ngugi wa Thiong'o.

Every effort has been made to trace the owners of copyright material
used in this book, but we should be pleased to hear from any
copyright holder whom we have been unable to contact.

We have made every effort to publish this book free of errors. Please
let us know if you notice any we have overlooked.
We would also be happy to receive your comments and suggestions,
and give you other information concerning our material.

Our address and fax number are:
Cideb Editrice – Piazza Garibaldi 11/2 – 16035 Rapallo (GE)
Fax 0185/230100 – e-mail: cidebedi@rapallo.newnetworks.it

ISBN 88-7754-328-0

Printed in Italy by Istituto Grafico Bertello, Borgo San Dalmazzo (CN)

Introduction, notes and activities by

R. A. HENDERSON

University of Turin

CIDEB

CONTENTS

INTRODUCTION

The Narrative Tradition

Telling and listening to stories seems to be one of the fundamental characteristics of human beings. Every culture has its traditional tales, often of heroes who save society from monstrous enemies; and although we no longer believe in the dragons of folk tales, stories about our own heroes and heroines – film stars, sports personalities, popular singers, fashion models and so on – fill our magazines and television shows. One of the attractions of these stories is that they give us an insight into ways of life which we may never experience directly; and this is something which fiction, too, can offer to the reader.

Because the short story has developed as a form dealing more with character and atmosphere than with action, it is particularly suited to this function. Although many people now travel extensively, a tourist's first-hand knowledge of a culture, visited for a few weeks under special circumstances (hotels, chartered aircraft, selected sightseeing) is still very limited. If we want to know what life is like in Nigeria or India or New Zealand, we must either live in these countries for an extended period or listen to what a native can tell us about them. The short stories collected here give us an opportunity to listen to natives of four different Continents talking about aspects of their own cultures.

Stories have been a part of literature for hundreds of years. Boccaccio's *Decameron* and Chaucer's *Canterbury Tales* are examples of collections of stories which were enormously successful in the Middle Ages; and at a time when few books were available and not many people knew how to read, many more stories must have circulated in oral form. With widespread education, the demand for reading material grew: the novel, with its complicated plots, detailed descriptions and often huge cast of characters, developed in the eighteenth and nineteenth centuries, at the very time when literacy was becoming the norm among the middle classes.

The Short Story

It was in the nineteenth century that the short story emerged as a separate genre, above all with Edgar Allan Poe, whose stories first appeared in the newly popular magazines which were entering many American homes in the 1830s. Poe's definition of the short story, as a narrative which can be read at one sitting in less than two hours, and which concentrates on a single effect, can hardly be bettered. The form was adopted in many languages: Guy de Maupassant in France and Anton Chekhov in Russia, both late nineteenth-century writers, are widely recognised as its greatest masters.

A short story may be told from various points of view. The first-person narrator, usually a character in the story, refers to her/himself as 'I'; the third-person narrator refers to all the characters as 'he/she/they'. Third-person narrators may be impersonal, telling the story without comment, or intrusive, supplying a guiding commentary to shape the reader's reaction; they may identify with a single character whose thoughts and feelings are displayed to the reader, or take an omniscient standpoint, knowing and revealing every character's thoughts. What all short stories have in common is economy: of plot, of characters and of narration.

Across the World

Although technology and transport have made the world seem much smaller, most of us remain rooted in a single, fairly limited culture. It is interesting to notice how, as the idea of a united Europe has taken form, the sense of local identity has become increasingly important, leading at times to conflict between countries, regions and ethnic groups. The manifestations of this phenomenon are of various kinds: separatist movements may have recourse to terrorism, as has happened in Northern Spain and in Ireland; there may be an outbreak of civil war, as in Bosnia; representatives may adopt an identifying uniform and establish symbolic rituals, as in the case of the Italian Northern League; or a political solution may be found, as in the recent referendum for a separate Scottish Assembly within the United Kingdom. It is nevertheless clear that the various races that constitute Europe have more in common, in many ways, with each other than with peoples on other Continents, where striking differences may range from physical appearance to standards of correct behaviour. Social and economic circumstances, the natural environment and the impact of colonising settlers have all played their part in making life in India or Africa or Australia what it is today.

The most significant contribution of the colonisers has been the imposition of their own languages: French, Spanish and English are all spoken today as first or official languages of countries on other Continents. This is something of a two-edged sword: a shared language makes communication easier, but may at the same time mask important differences. As Tom McArthur points out in his *Oxford Companion to the English Language*, 'all the national standards [of English] are close to one another': thus an educated Australian will have no difficulty in understanding an educated Indian, and vice versa. Nevertheless, every speech community brings new words and

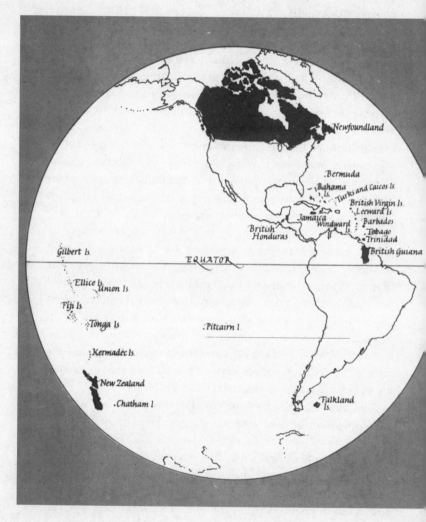

The British Empire in 1897.

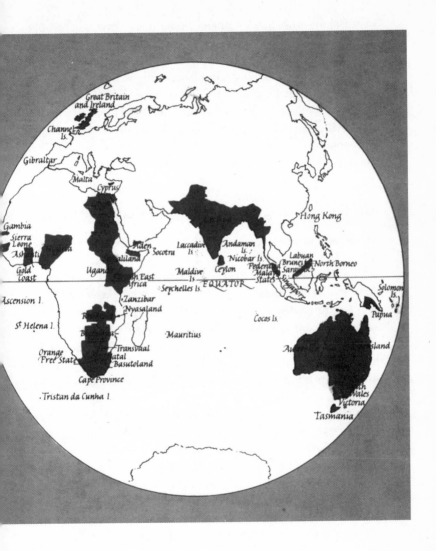

expressions into the language. Sometimes these are simply borrowed from other local languages to identify something – an animal, a plant, a kind of food – for which there is no English word; sometimes they are modifications of the grammar or pronunciation of English in the direction of the local language. Differences of this kind will be particularly apparent among the less educated classes, and will be more noticeable in conversation than in writing; in fiction, they are reflected in dialogue rather than in description or narration.

The English Language and the Four Continents

There used to be a popular saying that 'the sun never sets on the British Empire', because British imperial governments had been established all over the world: in Africa, in North America, in Asia and in Australasia. Then the Empire was transformed into the Commonwealth, an association of independent, self-governing states, including Britain; subsequently a number of states withdrew from the Commonwealth, but there are still 49 members with a total population of more than one thousand million. In all these countries, as well as those which were formerly under British rule, English is widely used. Of the countries represented in this volume, English is the first language of the majority of the population in Australia, Canada, New Zealand and Trinidad; it is the official language, or one of the official languages, in all the others except Kenya. This is why writers from the four Continents can choose English as their literary medium, even though they may habitually speak and write at least one other tongue. There are obvious advantages in the use of a language which is as widespread as English: from the commercial point of view alone, it is clear that more copies will be sold of a book in English than of a book in, say, Dutch or Swahili. At the same time, a language shared by nations with very different religious beliefs, social organisations and ways of life can be deceptive, masking the differences in such a way that readers from another culture may mistakenly perceive the world of the writer as similar to their own. We must be alert to this possibility in approaching the stories in this volume.

There is a further point to be borne in mind. Attitudes to the English language itself vary from country to country, from individual to individual. For some writers, finding readers all over the world is an advantage which outweighs the possibility of misunderstanding just suggested. On the Indian sub-continent there are at least fourteen major regional languages, many of them virtually unknown outside India; a story written in one of these languages cannot be expected to have much impact on the rest of the world. This, as I have said, is a matter of economics for the professional writer; but it is also a question of communicating ideas, and ideals, to other cultures. There are, on the other hand, writers who feel that the English language is the instrument of a kind of cultural tyranny, and who consequently reject it: Ngugi wa Thiong'o, whose story *Minutes Of Glory* is included in this volume, no longer uses English as the medium for his creative writing. The sense of English as an irrelevance or an intrusion is naturally stronger in countries where the majority of the population are not of British descent, or among ethnic groups of indigenous peoples like the Maoris in Witi Ihimaera's *A Game Of Cards*; but an analogous attitude can be detected in communities of immigrants in English-speaking countries, such as the Jews in Mordecai Richler's *The Summer My Grandmother Was Supposed To Die* or the Sikhs in Khushwant Singh's *When Sikh Meets Sikh*. This is why, though it is still appropriate to talk of such stories as being written in English, they include many words and expressions unfamiliar to native speakers of English from other communities.

Nine Countries

This is not the place for a detailed history of how European settlers arrived in distant countries and affected their development; but a few notes on the subject will provide background for the stories which follow. Since explorers – above all from Great Britain, Italy and Spain – began to discover, in the 16th century, that there were regions of the world whose existence had been unsuspected, colonies of immigrant Europeans have been established in almost every habitable area, with sometimes disastrous consequences for the indigenous cultures. The newcomers seem always to have assumed that their own way of life was superior to any other, and that by imposing their standards and ideas they were doing an immense favour to the local peoples, whose religious beliefs and social organisation were relegated to a subordinate place, if not actually destroyed. Inevitably, this meant either that the natives submitted to the elimination of their culture, or that they engaged in an often violent struggle to maintain it in the face of the colonisers' opposition.

In Australia, the aboriginal population was at best neglected, at worst attacked and exploited by the newcomers – indeed, in Tasmania, totally eliminated – and they are still regarded as inferior by many New Australians. Australian literature is almost entirely concerned with the white population: in the recent past, few writers have even mentioned the aborigines, Xavia Herbert being the most significant exception. Today, more than half the total population of Australia is concentrated in four large cities: Perth in the west, Adelaide in the south, Sydney and Melbourne on the east coast. There are still vast areas of the Continent which are only sparsely inhabited; some of these are difficult or impossible to cultivate, while others provide grazing for sheep on a scale unimaginable to Europeans. Before the technological advances which made it possible to cover many

Aboriginals with traditional hunting boomerangs and spears.

hundreds of square miles of territory in a relatively short time, this kind of farming led to the isolation of the stockmen who were responsible for the day-to-day care of the animals: forced, at times, to live for long periods far from their families, they developed an all-male solidarity which is reflected in the literature of the late 19th and early 20th centuries. The rural communities thus formed were the source of a vigorous folk culture which found expression in their songs and stories.

The situation in New Zealand is somewhat different. When the first white settlers arrived there, they found an advanced and complex culture among the indigenous Maoris; and although European influence has not been entirely beneficial,

An ancient Maori canoe.

the Maoris have maintained their identity and are actually multiplying faster than New Zealanders of European stock. There are, in effect, two parallel cultures in New Zealand, living in close proximity – for the total area of New Zealand is very much less than that of Australia. The Maoris continue to live according to traditions established long before the arrival of the white settlers; and the immigrants follow a way of life which has been defined as 'more English than England'. There is occasional conflict, but on the whole the two communities have learned to coexist peaceably.

Nelson Mandela voting in the 1994 general elections.

The same cannot be said of the African countries, where tension between the native and immigrant populations has often led to violence and discrimination. It was above all the long imprisonment of Nelson Mandela that drew attention in Europe to the appalling injustice of apartheid, the South African law forbidding any association between blacks and whites. Intermarriage was illegal; blacks could not eat in the same restaurants or sit in the same cinemas and theatres as whites; they had little opportunity for education, and were thus kept firmly in a subordinate position as the servants – almost slaves – of the ruling white population. Many white South Africans sincerely believed that blacks were ineducable, that they would be incapable of managing their own affairs and must be protected from their own base instincts. They treated their black employees rather as they treated children or domestic animals: not necessarily brutally, but on the assumption that they were by nature inferior beings. It is only in the last few years that the situation has been rectified, and it remains difficult, if not impossible, for many white South Africans to believe that the native blacks are entitled to, and capable of administering, their independence.

Elsewhere in Africa, although there has never been a formal apartheid law, conflict between white and black, and between warring tribes of blacks, has been a recurrent problem. The granting of self-government to countries like Nigeria or Kenya, while it was an overdue recognition of the rights of the indigenous peoples to control their own destiny, often created new difficulties in the attempt to reconcile the old way of life with the new. Many of the political leaders of the new Africa

African women going to the market.

had been educated in European universities; they had absorbed British ideas which did not always sit easily with the expectations of their own nations. The sometimes intrusive presence of Christian missionaries was a source of further problems: there was a tendency to suppress the traditional beliefs of the Africans rather than allowing them to adapt in the direction of the Christian church. The results have been, in some cases, explosions of violence and the rejection of everything that represented the colonisers, from their language to their administrative systems and their creed. All this is reflected in the writings of African authors such as Chinua Achebe and Ngugi wa Thiong'o.

There is tension in Canada, too, but of a rather different kind: this part of the North American Continent was colonised twice over, by the French and the British, with the result that there are two distinct language communities among the descendants of the colonisers. French and English are both official languages (used, that is, by national and local administration, the mass media and educational bodies at all levels); the languages of the indigenous peoples have no official status. Those Canadian writers who choose to write in English have a further choice to make: with the United States its nearest neighbour, Canada is subject to strong American influence, but many Canadians insist upon their British connections and hence upon the use of British spelling and vocabulary, where these vary from the standard American forms.

Finally, in the West Indies, yet another situation prevails. The population there is a rich intermingling of ethnic groups: the descendants of African, Indian and white European immigrants live side by side and have each made their contribution to the varieties of English spoken (and written) in the Caribbean. Many West Indians – including the two authors represented here, from the independent island states of Trinidad and Dominica – have, in their turn, emigrated to Europe, where their loyalty to their native islands has led to the establishment of imported traditions in a number of British cities: the annual Notting Hill Carnival in London is an example. It is worth noting that the two West Indian stories chosen for this volume, though written in England, are set in the Caribbean, the childhood environment of their authors.

Scholars differ about the future of the English language worldwide: will varieties emerge in different countries with so many distinctive features that they are, in effect, separate languages? The resulting situation might be rather like the relationship between, say, Welsh and Breton today: speakers of these two Celtic tongues can understand each other, but it is generally agreed that there *are* two separate tongues, and not just two different dialects. At present, the position is a particularly happy one: anyone who knows English has access to a vast range of literary (and other) materials which, though they come from many cultures, present no serious difficulties of understanding; and this, in its turn, means that we can explore each other's cultures through our shared language.

The Bridegroom

The white population of South Africa was accustomed for many years to consider the black races inferior in every way. No account was taken of their rights in their own land: white settlers from the Netherlands and from Great Britain had brought the fruits of their industrialised civilisation to these technologically primitive peoples, and believed that this gave them the exclusive right to all kinds of privileges. At worst, they treated the blacks like animals; at best, like children.

The young man in Nadine Gordimer's story belongs to the second category. By virtue of his white skin, he has a position of official superiority, in charge of 'a gang of kaffirs': he is the only white man in the road camp, and there is no other white person

Anti-apartheid demonstrators in South Africa.

less than fourteen miles away. He is engaged to be married, having – with some difficulty – convinced his seventeen-year-old fiancée's parents that 'the life [is] not impossible', despite the two hundred and twenty miles dividing them from the nearest town or village, and the fact that she will be completely isolated when he is out at work with his road gang. Meanwhile, he has developed a routine that gives him security, and a series of relationships with the members of his gang.

The most important of these relationships is with Piet, his 'boy'. (This is the term regularly used by European settlers in many African countries for their adult male servants; the implication of immaturity is suggestive of their attitude.) Piet cooks for the young man, keeps his tent clean and tidy (and it is 'neater than any house would ever be') – in short, he fulfils the duties traditionally associated with a housewife, making it difficult to imagine what role the seventeen-year-old girl will occupy besides that of sexual partner. The banter between Piet and his master is strongly reminiscent of the confidential tone of many happily-married couples: Piet 'nags' the young man 'with deep satisfaction'; his laughter expresses 'pleasure in constancy to an old [joke]'; they pretend anger with each other, both knowing that it is only a game. So intimate is their understanding that they communicate even without words:

> 'You must do everything nice when the missus comes.'
> 'Baas?'
> They looked at each other and it was not really necessary to say anything. (p. 11)

Almost unconsciously, the young man has conferred on Piet the status of an equal: Piet shows no deference to his employer, but treats him – and is treated – as a friend.

There is repeated emphasis on the need for change which the bride's presence will bring:

> The boys must keep out of the way. That was the main thing . . . The women over there – they could do the washing for the girl . . . They just mustn't hang around, that's all. They must just understand that they mustn't hang around. (pp. 11-12)

> Piet, Piet, that kaffir talks such a hell of a lot. How's Piet going to stop talking, talking every time he comes near? If he talks to her . . . Man it's sure he'll talk to her. (p. 12)

> He sat for he was not aware how long, just as he had for so many other nights, with the stars at his head and the fire at his feet.
> But at last the music stopped and time began again. There was tonight; there was tomorrow, when he was going to drive to Francistown. (p. 17)

It is hard to escape the conclusion that the young man's marriage will bring him increased loneliness: that the evenings of shared music, of intimacy around the fire, will end with the arrival of his wife, whose presence will enforce a new separation within the community of the road gang.

Railway station in Dakar.

The Sacrificial Egg

The whole of this brief story is built on tension between the world of African tradition and the new rituals and beliefs of modern commerce. The office in Umuru, where Julius Obi works, is evidence that he has travelled, culturally speaking, much further than the 'twenty or so miles' separating the town from his native village: he has attended a mission school, where he has learned to abandon the superstitions of his people. Yet his new rationality is constantly challenged by everything around him: the market which is still busier on the day when its presiding deity casts her spell than on the other days imposed by 'the coming of the white man' and the demands of trade; the future mother-in-law who, although she is 'a very devout Christian' (like Julius himself), still talks about spirits from her pagan background; and, above all, the sacrificial egg of the title.

This kind of tension, born of confusion, is a familiar part of the experience of many educated Africans, like Achebe himself.

When an entire society has been built on a particular system of beliefs, objective probability is not the only, or even the best, criterion for that system's maintenance or rejection. Julius is an Ibo; to step on a sacrificial egg is, for him, to attract misfortune, and this is no more absurd than the idea, widespread in Western Europe, that breaking a mirror brings seven years' bad luck, or that our characters are determined by the position of the planets at the moment we are born. Indeed, Achebe's story invites us to suppose that the Ibo superstition is well grounded, for the breaking of the egg is followed by the deaths of Julius's fiancée and her mother.

The crucial moment is preceded and followed by further evidence that Julius is not so 'modern' as he would like to believe. He steps on the egg because he is hurrying to get home before the night spirit begins its race through the town; and shortly afterwards he hears 'the rattling staff of the spirit and a thundering stream of esoteric speech'. Is the spirit a reality? Julius clearly thinks so; we readers must make our own decision. Certainly the intensity of Achebe's writing is persuasive. The story is also a reminder of the power of epidemic diseases such as smallpox, a power as terrifying and uncontrollable as that of the Ibo spirits.

Minutes Of Glory

From the first lines of the story, Ngugi wa Thiong'o stresses the fragility of his protagonist's sense of her identity. 'Her name was Wanjiru. But she liked better her Christian one, Beatrice.' This girl, a victim of the poverty of her Third World country, struggles to re-create herself on the model of Nyagūthiī, the young woman she admires and envies for her apparently effortless success with men, because she is 'both totally immersed in and yet completely above the underworld of bar violence and sex' (p. 35). Beatrice looks for keys to a transformation of her appearance that will lead, in turn, to a transformation of her life: she even tries to lighten her black skin with commercial products, but she is still trapped in the world of beer-halls and casual prostitution, and has not even the strength to break her employer's rules as the other girls do, until he tries to take her to his own bed. Because of her rebellion Beatrice loses her job, and subsequently goes to work in a new, fashionable bar where she is a general servant, 'invisible' to the rich men who go there to drink and sleep.

When at last she finds a lover, he is 'the opposite of the lover of her dreams', not one of the wealthy patrons in their expensive cars, but a lorry driver. Through his attentions she makes a little money, but the relationship does not satisfy her. Beatrice's need for 'a human being who would understand' is not fulfilled by the self-pitying lorry driver, whom she finally forces to listen to her own pathetic story. But this does not bring her the expected relief, and she adopts a new identity, stealing her lover's money and using it to effect a short-lived transformation with new clothes and jewellery. For a few hours she is the centre of attention, controlling the men around her instead of being exploited by them, until she is arrested for theft. At once, her image is destroyed, and it is the lorry driver who becomes a 'hero'.

The brief conversation between Beatrice and Nyagũthiĩ immediately after the theft offers special insight into the predicament of African girls in the new townships, at the mercy of a materialism which, the writer seems to suggest, is colonialism's principal legacy. Nyagũthiĩ, from a relatively privileged background, has rebelled against repressive rules and has cut herself off from her family in her search for 'instant excitement'; yet she has maintained her capacity to recognise, in Beatrice, a quality she herself does not share, a personal dignity which, even as she acknowledges it, Beatrice knows she has lost. Beatrice's tragedy is that she abandons the one characteristic that marked her out as special; the irony of her situation is that she believes she can become special only if she conforms to the expectations of the community around her. By seeking a new identity she destroys Wanjiru, the essence of herself whom she has longed to deny. Her story is an indictment of one of the most negative consequences of colonisation: the sense many people have that to be African is to be inferior, and that white 'superiority' can be attained by aping all that is worst in Western European culture.

The Union Buries Its Dead

This account of a funeral runs counter to all our expectations. The dead man is accompanied to his grave by a small group of men whose only link with him is their membership of the same union. There is no grieving family, there are no flowers, there is no sense of reverence before the mystery of death; yet the fourteen union members take the time to go to the funeral out of a sense of solidarity with one of their kind. At least thirty others ('more than two thirds of the funeral') intend to go, but are drunk by the time the coffin arrives.

Lawson's story constantly reminds us of the poverty, in every sense, of the ceremony. Not only is the coffin covered with a cheap, shabby cloth, but the behaviour of the mourners demonstrates their inability to respond to the pathos of the situation: before the procession begins they drink and dance and fight; during the religious service they are ill at ease. None of them is identified by name: they are simply 'the union'.

This kind of community, where labour and drink are the priorities and there is strict segregation of men from women, was not uncommon in Australia in the first half of the twentieth century and indeed remains the norm in some remote rural areas. Australia was settled, in the nineteenth century, largely by convicts whose crimes made them undesirable members of society. Exportation to the other side of the world was a convenient way of reducing the prison population; but it led, inevitably, to the establishment in their new home of traditions based on the lower-class criminal culture from which many of them came. There was little room for sentimentality and little sense of the kind of values we have come to associate with 'civilisation': culture, education, sensitivity to others' feelings. Alcohol helped these men to forget their hard life; the unforgiving society that had trapped them on a vast, empty island far from home was bearable after a few beers. Lawson's characters are the inheritors of social injustice.

The grim humour of the story is disconcerting. Partly, this is achieved through the narrator's apparent detachment: he mentions no individual by name, and refers to the group, collectively, as 'it'. This deliberate suppression of individuality makes it impossible for the reader to become personally involved in the story. We accept the comedy because we remain at a distance from the young man's death; nevertheless, it is unusual to read an account of a funeral in which the keynote is a hilarious incongruousness. The hat held over the priest's head illustrates this: it has 'a conical crown and a brim sloping down

all round like a sunshade'. The mental picture evoked is very
funny.

Yet the last lines of the story invite serious reflection. Even
the young man's identity – as 'James Tyson' – is removed from
him, and his real name vanishes from the union members'
indifferent memories. It is as though, in the most absolute sense,
he had never existed.

The Persimmon Tree

One of the strengths of the short story is illustrated by this
example: it need not, in the ordinary sense, tell a story. Nothing
really happens in *The Persimmon Tree*; the author's purpose is to
create an atmosphere, and this she does through long
descriptive passages of great delicacy.

The narrator is convalescing after a long illness, and is in that
state of heightened sensibility which many people experience in
such circumstances. She is acutely conscious of her
surroundings: colour, shape and texture are particularly
important to her, and the intense colour of the persimmons
stands out in contrast to the understatement of the rest of her
descriptions. Significantly, they are mentioned before the figure
of the woman across the street is seen – the woman who is to
become so important to the narrator, but who is never brought
before the reader as vividly as the fruit she sets out on her
windowsill. There is no sense of curiosity about her: she is given
no name; we are told nothing about 'the texture of her skin, her
hands, the set of her clothes, her movements' apart from the
deliberately vague 'long dark wrap' she is wearing in the last
part of the story. All the detail in the narrative is devoted to
nature: the trees that line the street, the persimmons, the plants
growing in the bowl on the windowsill. In this sense Marjorie
Barnard is writing in the tradition of Romanticism, where nature
takes on the role of protagonist, as teacher and comforter.

The Summer My Grandmother Was Supposed To Die

Although on one level this is a comedy, the predicament at the centre of the story is a painful one. The narrator's family is faced with the problem of an elderly relative whose health is slowly deteriorating but who survives as a helpless invalid for several years. What is best for the old lady? What is best for the rest of the family?

The story is told by a child, with the result that Richler is able to maintain a certain emotional distance from the dying woman. For Muttel, six years old when his grandmother is taken ill, her speechless presence in the house is a source of fear and resentment: unlike his mother, he has no memories of happier times and no sense of responsibility to the dying woman, but sees her as an obstacle to his independence (he is forced to share a room with his brother Harvey as long as his grandmother occupies the back bedroom) and as something less than human. As he grows and develops, so she declines, becoming increasingly remote from the urgencies of the boy's world.

Muttel is also a filter for the account of the growing tension between his parents. Because he is too young to appreciate all the complexities of the situation, he does not take sides; and this allows the reader to view the situation with a certain objectivity. At no point does Richler show a marked preference for either parent's point of view; rather, he shows the weaknesses and strengths of both sides, leaving it to us to make our own choices. The father's concern is above all for his wife: with unsentimental dryness he makes it clear that this is a physical and emotional burden which is putting her health at risk. The mother is torn between exhaustion ('It's killing me', she admits at one point) and devotion to what the old lady represents – a memory of lifelong care and affection. This kind of dilemma is increasingly common in Western society.

What makes Richler's story different is, above all, the Jewish background. Jews tend to have a particularly strong sense of family solidarity; in addition, in many countries they live in closed communities, bound together by their shared history of persecution and rootlessness as well as by their religious and cultural traditions. This strengthens family bonds, since the broader social context is relatively limited. But living within another, less restricted community leads inevitably to the adoption of ideas and attitudes from that larger context, which is why Muttel's aunts and uncles do not share his mother's sense of absolute family duty.

The humour of much of the dialogue may surprise some readers in a story about death, for Richler views his community with a satirical but not unfriendly eye. The mother's grief at the end of the story is sensitively reported, but the last word goes to an uncle who is already thinking ahead to the future of the two boys: ' "Well, boys," he said, "what would you like to be when you grow up?" '.

When Sikh Meets Sikh

Unlike many of the stories collected here, this one gives the reader some essential background information. The first four paragraphs tell us about the beliefs of Sikhs, about their attitudes and about their versatility; it is thus possible to see Nanjo as a product of a specific culture.

The main action takes place in a wrestling ring, where the fighters conform to the expectations of their public. Neither their fighting nor their personalities while wrestling are genuine: Nanjo turns to Mecca 'as Canadians thought he should', and the spectators, for all their enthusiasm, know that the violence between the two men is only pretended ('phoney'). Even the end of the match, when Nanjo seems to have half-killed his opponent, is shown to be harmless: in the dressing room, Nanjo and Mazurki are 'the best of friends'.

As the story draws to an end, we discover the extent of Nanjo's loyalty to his origins: his plan is to go home and work as a farmer, taking his Canadian wife with him. As a 'buxom blonde', she will be obviously foreign in an Indian community, but she is already preparing for her new life by taking her husband's religion and learning a few words of his language. Singh suggests that adaptability can work in both directions: the first white settlers on the Indian sub-continent imposed their language and their way of life on the native population; but the message of Nanjo and his marriage is that immigrants, white or coloured, can and should accept the standards of their adopted community.

The Only American From Our Village

The construction of this story is worth careful attention. Within a frame provided by a brief general account of a distinguished scientist's life before and after his return visit to his home in India, the central episode is narrated. This episode – the scientist's meeting with an old man – is itself the frame for a further narrative: the old man's account of the scientist's father. Arun Joshi achieves remarkable depth with this complex structure, without abandoning the economy characteristic of the short story.

The title is a reminder of the legendary status America has achieved in many parts of the world. If we no longer believe that the streets there are paved with gold, still many young people on other Continents see the United States as a land of opportunity, where talent and industry are regularly rewarded with success in terms of both money and fame. This is exactly what has happened to Dr. Khanna: far from his native India, he has become 'the most outstanding immigrant physicist at the University of Wisconsin' and 'among the dozen or so best-dressed men on the campus'. He has married an American ('Joanne' is not an Indian name) and fathered two sons in the fifteen years since his emigration.

His visit to India takes on the appearance of a royal progress: he associates with important public figures, he gives lectures and seminars, and distributes gifts to the relatives whose circumstances are still modest. Joshi makes an ironic point with these gifts: 'Gillette razors, pop records and a mass of one-dollar neckties', none of them of immediate use to the recipients, who nevertheless 'worship' the Khanna family as though they had come down from heaven. There is a strong suggestion that neither the Americans nor the Indians are fully aware of the insensitivity lying behind the choice of such unsuitable gifts.

It is the poor man, the *ashtamp farosh*, who cuts through this dishonesty. His lengthy account of his old friend, Dr. Khanna's father, is hardly interrupted: he seems almost to have hypnotised the scientist, who listens to him helplessly and even submits to being touched by this unlovely figure ('The *ashtamp farosh* put his hand on Dr. Khanna's shoulder', p. 121). The story he tells is a sharp reminder of the physicist's good fortune: his intelligence is inherited from his father, but it has given him privileges undreamed of in earlier generations. As a son, however, he is a failure. It seems that it has never occurred to him to pay for his father to visit him in America; he excuses himself on the grounds that he 'did not have the money', but this is unconvincing from a man in his circumstances. Moreover, the *ashtamp farosh* tells him that his father had invested heavily in the expected invitation, buying shirts, a suit, a razor and a cake of soap. The significance of this is underlined by the earlier remark that none of Dr. Khanna's Indian relatives had suits, but that the razors he brought them 'were greatly prized'.

It seems, in the last lines of the story, that Dr. Khanna's return journey across the ocean has taken on, for him, a parallel significance to his father's last walk across the *cho*: the burning feet that at last link father and son are, for both men, the consequence of a kind of madness. For Dr. Khanna, there is also a suggestion of a kind of penance for his neglect of the responsibilities implicit in family ties.

A Horse And Two Goats

With the growth of mass tourism, encounters like the one in this story are increasingly frequent. The American, rich enough to travel for pleasure and entirely well-meaning, finds himself at cross-purposes with the old goat-keeper whom he meets at the foot of a statue. For the American, the statue is an artefact, a desirable object that would be the perfect souvenir of his visit to India; for the old man, it is a representation of part of his faith, inseparable from its immediate context. What the two men share is a preoccupation with money: the American is willing to spend a sum which for the old man represents unimaginable wealth. The comedy of their meeting arises from the fact that they have nothing else in common: neither language, nor education, nor cultural expectations. It does not occur to the old man that the American might want to buy the statue, as it does not occur to the American that the old man might believe that he has found a buyer for his goats.

Narayan never labours his point. It is left to the reader to imagine a series of hilarious possibilities, from the installation of the statue in a New York apartment to the still more improbable and at least equally unsuitable transfer of the goats to an American skyscraper. The humour of the situation applies in the same measure to both men: they are polite to each other, they do their best to communicate across the language barrier, they each believe that agreement has been reached to the satisfaction of both. Only the reader is in the privileged position of seeing the absurdity of the situation. There is special skill in the author's presentation of the old man's lengthy discourse on the symbolic significance of the statue: because it is rooted in Hindu beliefs, it is largely incomprehensible to a reader from another culture, even without the linguistic impenetrability that faces the American, but the dignity of the old man's faith comes through. There is, too, a subtle irony in the contrast between the poverty of the village and the grandeur of its projected future:

'At the end of this Kali Yuga, this world will be destroyed, and all the worlds will be destroyed, and it is then that the Redeemer will come, in the form of a horse called Kalki, and help the good people, leaving the evil ones to perish in the great deluge. And this horse will come to life then, and that is why this is the most sacred village in the whole world.' (p. 139)

Money gives the American a certain power, but even if he were able to buy the statue he could not enter into possession of the promise it embodies. Its value for the old man and his fellow-villagers is immeasurably greater than the American can imagine.

The fact that the statue is of an animal has further significance. Animals are the source of the old man's material livelihood as well as of his spiritual well-being. The American thinks of the goats as 'pets'; the old man sees them as a promise of capital. The two men are as far apart in their response to the goats as in their interpretation of the horse: it is the statue, not the living animals, that has emotional value for the old man, while the American believes the reverse. Narayan ends his story at a moment of comic suspense; it is up to the reader to decide how the impasse can be resolved.

Good Advice Is Rarer Than Rubies

The basis for this story is the widespread assumption that young people from Third World countries are eager to emigrate in search of prosperity. Rushdie's protagonists are both, in a sense, products of this idea: Muhammad Ali has made a career of advising aspiring emigrants on how to deal with the bureaucracy surrounding their applications, and Miss Rehana, as he expects, has come to ask for a permit to go to England. Rushdie makes it clear that the kind of interview Muhammad Ali initiates with the girl is, for him, a matter of routine; what makes this occasion unusual is the applicant herself.

Miss Rehana is exceptional in a number of ways: she is beautiful, she has exquisite manners, she has an air of independence – among the women visiting the British Consulate on this particular Tuesday, she is the only one to have come alone. All this is enough to make an impression on Muhammad Ali; but this young woman has other qualities that he does not suspect. Although she seems naive, it is she who is manipulating Muhammad Ali, and not – as he believes – the other way about; and although it seems obvious (to the reader as well as to the 'advice expert') that she wants to escape from a life of poverty in India, she has her own reasons for seeing matters differently.

One of the points Rushdie emphasises is the increasing difficulty of maintaining certain cultural traditions in a world where the right to individual liberty is generally recognised, especially among the young. Miss Rehana's parents – like Muhammad Ali – take it for granted that the kind of arranged marriage which has for centuries been a part of Indian culture will be acceptable to a girl at the end of the twentieth century. This is not quite so remote from our own society as we may think: in the 16th and early 17th centuries, it was regarded as normal for a girl's parents to choose her husband, sometimes without the couple's ever meeting before their marriage. Shakespeare's Juliet is the victim of precisely this idea: her father decides that she will marry the man of his choice, and is outraged when she shows reluctance; but whereas Juliet knows she cannot marry Paris because she is secretly in love with Romeo, Miss Rehana's reason is much less romantic. She shows great maturity in her assessment of the situation: she understands the risks of marriage in a strange country to a man twenty-one years her senior who is 'like a stranger' to her. The paradox is that this young woman, who has gone beyond the assumption of female inferiority at the basis of Indian society, is perhaps the only visitor to the Consulate that day who is happy to remain in that society.

The conclusion of the story shows with remarkable delicacy how great a gift Muhammad Ali has unwittingly given to Miss Rehana; and Rushdie's last words are for the old man who has offered her something 'rarer than rubies', fulfilling the role of 'advice expert' as never before 'in his long, hot, hard, unloving life'.

The Hole That Jack Dug

Sargeson's use of a highly colloquial style gives the reader the impression not only of directness but of sincerity: Tom, the narrator, has no reason to lie, and the simplicity and informality of his language suggest that he is in no sense sophisticated. The story revolves around the apparently pointless digging of a large hole, but is really an oblique account of a marriage between an ill-assorted couple: Jack, a manual labourer, and his 'missis', who has some pretensions to an intellectual life, represented by her having read 'more than ten books by an author called Hugh Walpole' (p. 166).

Her choice of reading matter is particularly interesting. Hugh Walpole (1884-1941) was born in New Zealand, but lived in Britain from the age of five and achieved popularity with a series of historical novels set in Cumberland, in North-West England. There seems to be a suggestion here that Mrs Parker yearns for a world which is distant in both time and space from the one she actually inhabits; certainly she is ill at ease with her husband's physicality and is embarrassed at his intrusion into her Saturday afternoon tea-party:

> . . . he grinned round at the company, looking awfully hairy and sweaty though not too naked on account of his dark colour, and even spouted one of his pieces of poetry (which his missis tried several times to interrupt) . . . (p. 169)

Significantly, Jack's friend Tom 'never got past the first chapter' of a book by Hugh Walpole (who was not, it should be said, a very 'difficult' writer), but is an admirer of Henry Lawson, the Australian author whose story *The Union Buries Its Dead* is included in this volume – and Lawson, as we have seen, deals with the kind of all-male, unintellectual community in which Jack and Tom spend their working life.

Jack is represented as both literally and figuratively down to earth: he shares none of his wife's social ambitions, and his job in the quarry, like his spare-time activity in the garden, brings him into direct contact with the earth. At the same time, through his conversations with his wife, Sargeson shows him to be capable of subtlety and humour. Simplicity is not to be confused with stupidity. Tom twice suggests, at the beginning and at the end of the story, that Jack is not altogether sane:

> [His eyes] always have a bit of a crazy look about them, and even though Jack is my closest cobber I will say that he'll do some crazy things. (p. 165)

> As for me, I'm ready to stick up for Jack any time. Though I don't say his missis is making a mistake when she says that some day he'll end up in the lunatic asylum. (p. 173)

The reader, however, is likely to see matters rather differently. One of the achievements of this little story is to leave the issue open despite the use of a far from objective first-person narrator.

A Game Of Cards

The response to Nanny Miro's death, which is the focal point of the story, is a triumph of community life. For many of us in the industrialised countries, the four walls of the family home enclose the only community we know. The architecture of our cities, with little space for contact among neighbours, makes it difficult for us to establish communal relationships; material wealth and the desire to protect it are a further stimulus to maintain our privacy. Death is sometimes referred to as 'the last taboo' in Western European society; this is equally true of many parts of America, Australia and New Zealand.

In this last country, however, the Maoris have continued to live in village communities which function like large families (the principle is the same as in Israeli *kibbutzim*, but the Maori tradition is much more long-standing). In this situation, every individual is cherished by the whole group and death is a shared experience. When the narrator of Ihimaera's story comes home from the city, the first thing his father tells him is that Nanny Miro is very sick; yet Nanny Miro, we immediately discover, is not a blood relative:

> Everybody used to say I was her favourite mokopuna, and that she loved me more than her own children . . . (p. 179)

The tie is strong enough for the young man to go straight to Nanny Miro's house as soon as he has left his luggage at home. This house, one of the largest in the village, is sketched in a few words: it is 'a big treasure house', and a natural gathering place for the women of the community. The friendly squabbling between Nanny Miro and her friend Mrs Heta is repetitive and childlike; it is also – which is more important – intimate and affectionate. The two women are close enough to exchange insults without offence; indeed, they take pleasure in their quarrels.

The simplicity of the language used, by the narrator as by the other characters, is particularly striking. A great deal of the dialogue is punctuated with exclamation marks, giving a sense of emotional energy:

> 'When you coming to pick up your hoha kids! They're wrecking the place!' (p. 180)

'You just keep your eyes to yourself, Maka tiko bum!'
(p. 181)

'But I know you! I bet you lost it all on poker!' (p. 183)

This is a community where feelings are close to the surface,
expressed vigorously, without reserve, so that elaborate
language is unnecessary; yet the deepest emotions find only
indirect expression: it is her friends' presence at Nanny Miro's
bedside that shows their love for her, as it is Mrs Heta's
extraordinary gesture of playing patience on the dead woman's
coffin that makes the reader aware of the depth of her grief.

Bogart

Like *The Summer My Grandmother Was Supposed To Die*, this story
is told from the point of view of a very young person. The man
known as Bogart has a powerful image in the small world he
inhabits. He is a creature of extremes: 'the most bored man I
ever knew'; 'quite the most popular man in the street'; 'a man of
mystery'; 'the most feared man in the street'. He achieves this
contradictory reputation by remaining detached from the life of
the street: not only is he taciturn and solitary, but he has
appeared without warning and, just as unexpectedly, he
disappears at intervals, returning each time with a modified
image, increasingly Americanised.

Naipaul, himself a thoroughly Anglicised West Indian who
has spent almost all his adult life in Britain, recognises the
absurdity of his protagonist's pretensions. Bogart is clearly a
simple man, of limited education but considerable cunning, who
can adapt to any circumstances – if he is to be believed, he has
been a sailor, a cowboy and a brothel-keeper in quick
succession, though the police account is somewhat different.
What is clear is that Bogart has made money – how, exactly, we

are never told. He is arrested for bigamy, but there is nothing to suggest that he has broken the law in other ways except his own boast about 'running the best brothel' in a town in Brazil, for 'judges and doctors and big-shot civil servants'.

His friends on the street, especially Hat, remain loyal to him, seeing him as a model of machismo. It is worth noticing that women remain marginal throughout the story: they are prostitutes, passers-by, deserted wives, but without individuality and, it seems, without rights. Hat's final defence of Bogart is that he has left the mother of his child 'to be a man, among we men'. Among the poor people of Miguel Street, male supremacy is perhaps the only kind of dignity these men can aspire to; but the price Bogart pays for it is significant. This 'hard-boiled' local hero ends the story in prison.

I Used To Live Here Once

Once again, we are invited here to reflect on the power of memory. The unnamed protagonist of this story constantly compares her surroundings – the river, the road, the house she used to live in – with her recollection of them; changes are apparent all around her, but recognition is immediate and makes her feel 'extraordinarily happy'. What has changed is the family occupying the house.

Jean Rhys is dealing here with the instability of human experience. The familiarity of the stepping stones, of the steps leading up to the house, of the trees and the lawn, are undermined by the rejection experienced by the woman when she approaches the two children. Though the natural environment is outwardly the same, she no longer has any claim on it except the claim of memory. It belongs, now, to the fair-haired children and their family.

PHONETIC SYMBOLS

Vowels

[ɪ]	*as in*	six
[i]	"	happy
[iː]	"	see
[e]	"	red
[æ]	"	hat
[ɑː]	"	car
[ɒ]	"	dog
[ɔː]	"	door
[ʊ]	"	put
[uː]	"	food
[ʌ]	"	cup
[ə]	"	about
[ɜː]	"	girl

Diphthongs

[eɪ]	*as in*	made
[aɪ]	"	five
[aʊ]	"	house
[ɔɪ]	"	boy
[əʊ]	"	home
[ɪə]	"	beer
[eə]	"	hair
[ʊə]	"	poor

Consonants

[b]	*as in*	bed
[k]	"	cat
[tʃ]	"	church
[d]	"	day
[f]	"	foot
[g]	"	good
[dʒ]	"	page
[h]	"	how
[j]	"	yes
[l]	"	leg
[m]	"	mum
[n]	"	nine
[ŋ]	"	sing
[p]	"	pen
[r]	"	red
[s]	"	soon
[z]	"	zoo
[ʃ]	"	show
[ʒ]	"	measure
[t]	"	tea
[θ]	"	thin
[ð]	"	this
[v]	"	voice
[w]	"	wine

[']   represents primary stress in the syllable which follows

[,]   represents secondary stress in the syllable which follows

[ᵣ]   indicates that the final 'r' is only pronounced before a
word beginning with a vowel sound (British English).
In American English, the 'r' is usually pronounced
before both consonants and vowel sounds.

Four Continents

Pre-reading Activities

1. What do you know about life in Africa, America, Asia and Australasia? Apart from obvious differences such as climate, clothing and diet, how do you expect people's lives to differ from one Continent to another? Do you believe there are certain values, attitudes and emotions which are universal? Which ones?

2. Have you already heard of any of the authors in this volume? Have you read any of their works?

3. Look at the list of titles. Are there some which excite your interest more than others? Which ones? What is it about these titles that attracts you? Can you explain why other titles do not interest you in the same way?

4. The English language, as you have studied it, is probably based on the standard form used by educated people in Britain. Are you aware of differences between British English and American English? What kinds of differences do you expect to find in the English language as it is used in other parts of the world? Is the social class of the speaker likely to be relevant?

5. In many of the stories in this volume, words from local languages are used without explanation from the author, although they may be unfamiliar to readers from other language communities, where it may be difficult to discover their meaning. (Some of these words have not been translated in the notes, so that you will have the same experience in reading as a native English speaker.) Why do you think the authors chose to include these words in their stories?

6. There is great emphasis, in our contemporary world, on visual images: cinema, television, CD-ROM, the Internet etc. Can you think of anything which can be achieved in a written narrative but would be lost on screen?

Africa

These symbols indicate the beginning and end of the passages recorded on the cassette.

The Bridegroom

Nadine Gordimer

Nadine Gordimer 1923-

One of South Africa's most distinguished writers, Nadine Gordimer has won numerous literary awards, including the Booker Prize in Great Britain, the Malaparte Prize in Italy and, in 1991, the Nobel Prize for Literature. A member of the privileged white community, she was an outspoken critic of apartheid, the compulsory segregation of blacks from whites practised in South Africa until recently, and of political censorship. She has used her literary gifts to highlight the injustice of white supremacy in African countries: indeed, most of her work deals, directly or – as in the case of *The Bridegroom* – indirectly, with the political situation in her native country. She has also collaborated with a photographer, David Goldblatt, on two books on the same theme. Her broad humanitarian vision has ensured a wide reading public for her work, even among those who do not share her views.

HE CAME INTO HIS ROAD camp that afternoon for the last time. It was neater than any house would ever be; the sand raked smooth in the clearing, the water drums [1] under the tarpaulin, [2] the flaps of his tent closed against the heat. Thirty yards away a black woman knelt, pounding mealies, [3] and two or three children, grey with Kalahari dust, played with a skinny dog. Their shrillness was no more than a bird's piping in the great spaces in which the camp was lost.

Inside his tent, something of the chill of the night before always remained, stale but cool, like the air of a church. There was his iron bed, with its clean pillowcase and big kaross. There was his table, his folding chair with the red canvas seat, and the chest in which his clothes were put away. Standing on the chest was the alarm clock that woke him at five every morning and the photograph of a seventeen-year-old girl from Francistown whom he was going to marry. They had been there a long time, the girl and the alarm clock; in the morning when he opened his eyes, in the afternoon when he came off the job. But now this was the last time. He was leaving for Francistown in the Roads

---

1. *water drums* : large cylindrical containers for water.
2. *tarpaulin* [tɑːˈpɔːlɪn] : sheet of waterproof material used for protection.
3. *mealies* : South African name for maize.

Department ten-tonner, [1] in the morning; when he came back, the next week, he would be married and he would have with him the girl, and the caravan which the department provided for married men. He had his eye on her as he sat down on the bed and took off his boots; the smiling girl was like one of those faces cut out of a magazine. He began to shed his working overalls, a rind [2] of khaki stiff with dust that held his shape as he discarded it, and he called, easily and softly, *'Ou Piet, ek wag.'* But the bony black man with his eyebrows raised like a clown's, in effort, and his bare feet shuffling under the weight, was already at the tent with a tin bath in which hot water made a twanging tune as it slopped from side to side.

When he had washed and put on a clean khaki shirt and a pair of worn grey trousers, and streaked back his hair with sweet-smelling pomade, he stepped out of his tent just as the lid of the horizon closed on the bloody eye of the sun. It was winter and the sun set shortly after five; the grey sand turned a fading pink, the low thorn scrub [3] gave out spreading stains of lilac shadow that presently all ran together; then the surface of the desert showed pocked and pored, [4] for a minute or two, like the surface of the moon through a telescope, while the sky remained light over the darkened earth and the clean crystal pebble of the evening star shone. The campfires – his own and the black men's, over there – changed from near-invisible flickers of liquid colour to brilliant focuses of leaping tongues of light; it was dark. Every evening he sat like this through the short ceremony of the closing of the day, slowly filling his pipe, slowly easing his back round to the fire, yawning off the stiffness of his labour. Suddenly he gave a smothered giggle, to himself, of excitement.

---

1. *ten-tonner* : lorry weighing ten tons.
2. *rind* : hard outer covering (usually used of cheese or bacon).
3. *scrub* : low trees and bushes growing in an area where there is not much rain.
4. *pocked and pored* : marked with large and small hollows, as the skin on a human face may be.

Her existence became real to him; he saw the face of the photograph, posed against a caravan door. He got up and began to pace about the camp, alert to promise. He kicked a log farther into the fire, he called an order to Piet, he walked up towards the tent and then changed his mind and strolled away again. In their own encampment at the edge of his, the road gang [1] had taken up the exchange of laughing, talking, yelling, and arguing that never failed them when their work was done. Black arms gestured under a thick foam of white soap, there was a gasp and splutter as a head broke the cold force of a bucketful of water, the gleaming bellies of iron cooking pots were carried here and there in a talkative preparation of food. He did not understand much of what they were saying – he knew just enough Tswana [2] to give them his orders, with help from Piet and one or two others who understood his own tongue, Afrikaans [3] – but the sound of their voices belonged to this time of evening. One of the babies who always cried was keeping up a thin, ignored wail; the naked children were playing the chasing game that made the dog bark. He came back and sat down again at the fire, to finish his pipe.

After a certain interval (it was exact, though it was not timed by a watch, but by long habit that had established the appropriate lapse of time between his bath, his pipe, and his food) he called out, in Afrikaans, 'Have you forgotten my dinner, man?'

From across the patch of distorted darkness where the light of the two fires did not meet, but flung wobbling shapes and opaque, overlapping radiances, came the hoarse, protesting laugh that was, better than the tribute to a new joke, the pleasure in constancy to an old one.

1. *road gang* : group of men working together to construct or maintain roads.
2. *Tswana* ['tswɑːnə] : the language of the Bantu tribe in South Africa.
3. *Afrikaans* [afrɪ'kɑːns] : a Dutch-related language spoken in South Africa, especially by the white population.

Then a few minutes later: 'Piet! I suppose you've burned everything, eh?'

'Baas?'

'Where's the food, man?'

In his own time the black man appeared with the folding table and an oil lamp. He went back and forth between the dark and light, bringing pots and dishes and food, and nagging with deep satisfaction, in a mixture of English and Afrikaans. 'You want koeksusters, so I make koeksusters. You ask me this morning. So I got to make the oil nice and hot, I got to get everything ready . . . It's a little bit slow. Yes, I know. But I can't get everything quick, quick. You hurry tonight, you don't want wait, then it's better you have koeksusters on Saturday, then I'm got time in the afternoon, I do it nice . . . Yes, I think next time it's better . . .'

Piet was a good cook. 'I've taught my boy how to make everything', the young man always told people, back in Francistown. 'He can even make koeksusters', he had told the girl's mother, in one of those silences of the woman's disapproval that it was so difficult to fill. He had had a hard time, trying to overcome the prejudice of the girl's parents against the sort of life he could offer her. He had managed to convince them that the life was not impossible, and they had given their consent to the marriage, but they still felt that the life was unsuitable, and his desire to please and reassure them had made him anxious to see it with their eyes and so forestall, by changes, their objections. The girl was a farm girl, and would not pine for [1] town life, but, at the same time, he could not deny to her parents that living on a farm with her family around her, and neighbours only thirty or forty miles away, would be very different from living two hundred and twenty miles from a town or village, alone with him in a road camp 'surrounded by a

_____

1. *pine for* : think longingly of.

gang of kaffirs [1] all day', as her mother had said. He himself simply did not think at all about what the girl would do while he was out on the road; and as for the girl, until it was over, nothing could exist for her but the wedding, with her two little sisters in pink walking behind her, and her dress that she didn't recognise herself in, being made at the dressmaker's, and the cake that was ordered with a tiny china bride and groom in evening dress, on the top.

He looked at the scored [2] table, and the rim of the open jam tin, and the salt cellar with a piece of brown paper tied neatly over the broken top, and said to Piet, 'You must do everything nice when the missus [3] comes.'

'Baas?'

They looked at each other and it was not really necessary to say anything.

'You must make the table properly and do everything clean.'

'Always I make everything clean. Why you say now I must make clean . . .'

The young man bent his head over his food, dismissing him.

While he ate his mind went automatically over the changes that would have to be made for the girl. He was not used to visualizing situations, but to dealing with what existed. It was like a lesson learned by rote; he knew the totality of what was needed, but if he found himself confronted by one of the component details, he foundered: he did not recognise it or know how to deal with it. The boys must keep out of the way. That was the main thing. Piet would have to come to the caravan quite a lot, to cook and clean. The boys – especially the boys who were responsible for the maintenance of the lorries and road-making equipment – were always coming with questions, what to do about this and that. They'd mess things

---

1. *kaffirs* : a member of the Bantu tribe; in South Africa, often used as a negative term for black people generally.
2. *scored* : marked with shallow cuts.
3. *missus* ['mɪsəz] : (informal) wife.

up, otherwise. He spat out a piece of gristle [1] he could not swallow; his mind went to something else. The women over there – they could do the washing for the girl. They were such a raw [2] bunch of kaffirs, would they ever be able to do anything right? Twenty boys and above five of their women – you couldn't hide them under a thorn bush. They just mustn't hang around, that's all. They must just understand that they mustn't hang around. He looked round keenly through the shadow-puppets of the half-dark on the margin of his fire's light; the voices, companionably quieter, now, intermittent over food, the echoing *chut*! of wood being chopped, the thin film of a baby's wail through which all these sounded – they were on their own side. Yet he felt an odd, rankling [3] suspicion.

His thoughts shuttled, [4] as he ate, in a slow and painstaking way that he had never experienced before in his life – he was worrying. He sucked on a tooth; Piet, Piet, that kaffir talks such a hell of a lot. How's Piet going to stop talking, talking every time he comes near? If he talks to her . . . Man, it's sure he'll talk to her. He thought, in actual words, what he would say to Piet about this; the words were like those unsayable things that people write on walls for others to see in private moments, but that are never spoken in their mouths.

Piet brought coffee and koeksusters and the young man did not look at him.

But the koeksusters were delicious, crisp, sticky, and sweet, and as he felt the familiar substance and taste on his tongue, alternating with the hot bite of the coffee, he at once became occupied with the pure happiness of eating as a child is fully occupied with a bag of sweets. Koeksusters never failed to give him this innocent, total pleasure. When first he had taken the job

---

1. *gristle* ['grɪsəl] : stringy pieces in meat, which are difficult to chew.

2. *raw* : (here) inexperienced.

3. *rankling* : causing anger or bitterness.

4. *shuttled* ['ʃʌtəld] : moved back and forward.

of overseer to the road gang, he had had strange, restless hours at night and on Sundays. It seemed that he was hungry. He ate but never felt satisfied. He walked about all the time, like a hungry creature. One Sunday he actually set out to walk (the Roads Department was very strict about the use of the ten-tonner for private purposes) the fourteen miles across the sand to the cattle-dipping post [1] where the government cattle officer and his wife, Afrikaners like himself and the only other white people between the road camp and Francistown, lived in their corrugated-iron house. By a coincidence, they had decided to drive over and see him, that day, and they had met him a little less than halfway, when he was already slowed and dazed by heat. But shortly after that Piet had taken over the cooking of his meals and the care of his person, and Piet had even learned to make koeksusters, according to instructions given to the young man by the cattle officer's wife. The koeksusters, a childhood treat that he could indulge in whenever he liked, seemed to mark his settling down; the solitary camp became a personal way of life, with its own special arrangements and indulgences.

'*Ou Piet! Kèrel!* What did you do to the koeksusters, hey?' he called out joyously.

A shout came that meant 'Right away'. The black man appeared, drying his hands on a rag, with the diffident, kidding [2] manner of someone who knows he has excelled himself.

'Whatsa matter with the koeksusters, man?'

Piet shrugged. 'You must tell me. I don't know what's matter.'

'Here, bring me some more, man.' The young man shoved the empty plate at him, with a grin. And as the other went off, laughing, the young man called. 'You must always make them like that, see?'

---

1. *cattle-dipping post* : place where cows and bulls are put into a liquid containing disinfectant for a short time, to kill parasite insects living on their bodies.
2. *kidding* : joking, not serious.

He liked to drink at celebrations, at weddings or Christmas, but he wasn't a man who drank his brandy every day. He would have two brandies on a Saturday afternoon, when the week's work was over, and for the rest of the time, the bottle that he brought from Francistown when he went to collect stores lay in the chest in his tent. But on this last night he got up from the fire on impulse and went over to the tent to fetch the bottle (one thing he didn't do, he didn't expect a kaffir to handle his drink for him; it was too much of a temptation to put in their way). He brought a glass with him, too, one of a set of six made of tinted imitation cut glass, and he poured himself a tot [1] and stretched out his legs where he could feel the warmth of the fire through the soles of his boots. The nights were not cold, until the wind came up at two or three in the morning, but there was a clarifying chill to the air; now and then a figure came over from the black men's camp to put another log on the fire whose flames had dropped and become blue. The young man felt inside himself a similar low incandescence; he poured himself another brandy. The long yelping of the jackals [2] prowled the sky without, like the wind about a house; there was no house, but the sounds beyond the light of his fire tremblingly inflated into the dark – that jumble [3] of meaningless voices, crying babies, coughs, and hawking [4] – had built walls to enclose and a roof to shelter. He was exposed, turning naked to space on the sphere of the world as the speck that is a fly plastered on the window of an aeroplane, but he was not aware of it.

The lilt [5] of various kinds of small music began and died in the dark; threads of notes, blown and plucked, that disappeared under the voices. Presently a huge man whose thick black body

1. *tot* : small amount of strong alcoholic drink in a glass.
2. *jackals* ['dʒækɔːlz] : wild dogs found in South Africa.
3. *jumble* : disorganised mass.
4. *hawking* : clearing the throat noisily.
5. *lilt* : light, pleasant musical sound.

had strained apart every seam in his ragged pants and shirt loped [1] silently into the light and dropped just within it, not too near the fire. His feet, intimately crossed, were cracked and weathered [2] like driftwood. He held to his mouth a one-stringed instrument shaped like a lyre, made out of a half-moon of bent wood with a ribbon of dried palm leaf tied from tip to tip. His big lips rested gently on the strip and while he blew, his one hand, by controlling the vibration of the palm leaf, made of his breath a small, faint, perfect music. It was caught by the very limits of the capacity of the human ear; it was almost out of range. The first music men ever heard, when they began to stand upright among the rushes at the river, might have been like it. When it died away it was difficult to notice at what point it really had gone.

'Play that other one,' said the young man, in Tswana. Only the smoke from his pipe moved.

The pink-palmed hands settled down round the instrument. The thick, tender lips were wet once. The faint desolate voice spoke again, so lonely a music that it came to the player and listener as if they heard it inside themselves. This time the player took a short stick in his other hand and, while he blew, scratched it back and forth inside the curve of the lyre, where the notches [3] cut there produced a dry, shaking, slithering sound, like the far-off movement of dancers' feet. There were two or three figures with more substance than the shadows, where the firelight merged with the darkness. They came and squatted. One of them had half a paraffin tin, with a wooden neck and other attachments of gut [4] and wire. When the lyre-player paused, lowering his piece of stick and leaf slowly, in ebb [5], from his mouth, and wiping his lips on the back of his

1. *loped* : moved with long steps.
2. *weathered* : darkened by the effects of sun and rain.
3. *notches* : small cuts made in the surface.
4. *gut* : string made from part of the stomach of an animal.
5. *in ebb* : (here) as the sound grew fainter.

hand, the other began to play. It was a thrumming, repetitive, banjo tune. The young man's boot patted the sand in time to it and he took it up with hand-claps once or twice. A thin, yellowish man in an old hat pushed his way to the front past sarcastic remarks and twittings [1] and sat on his haunches with a little clay bowl between his feet. Over its mouth there was a keyboard of metal tongues. After some exchange, he played it and the others sang low and nasally, bringing a few more strollers to the fire. The music came to an end, pleasantly, and started up again, like a breath drawn. In one of the intervals the young man said, 'Let's have a look at that contraption [2] of yours, isn't it a new one?' and the man to whom he signalled did not understand what was being said to him but handed over his paraffin-tin mandolin with pride and also with amusement at his own handiwork.

The young man turned it over, twanged it once, grinning and shaking his head. Two bits of string and an old jam tin and they'll make a whole band, man. He'd heard them playing some crazy-looking things. The circle of faces watched him with pleasure; they laughed and lazily remarked to each other; it was a funny-looking thing, all right, but it worked. The owner took it back and played it, clowning a little. The audience laughed and joked appreciatively; they were sitting close in to the fire now, painted by it. 'Next week' the young man raised his voice gaily – 'next week when I come back, I bring radio with me, plenty real music. All the big white bands play over it . . .' Someone who had once worked in Johannesburg said, 'Satchmo', [3] and the others took it up, understanding that this was the word for what the white man was going to bring from town. Satchmo. Satch-

---

1. *twittings* : joking remarks made to irritate someone in a friendly way.

2. *contraption* : machine or device which seems strange to the speaker.

3. *Satchmo* : the nickname of the great American jazz musician Louis Armstrong (1900-71).

mo. They tried it out, politely. 'Music, just like at a big white dance in town. Next week.' A friendly, appreciative silence fell, with them all resting back in the warmth of the fire and looking at him indulgently. A strange thing happened to him. He felt hot, over first his neck, then his ears and his face. It didn't matter, of course; by next week they would have forgotten. They wouldn't expect it. He shut down his mind on a picture of them, hanging round the caravan to listen, and him coming out on the steps to tell them . . .

He thought for a moment that he would give them the rest of the bottle of brandy. Hell, no, man, it was mad. If they got the taste for the stuff, they'd be pinching it all the time. He'd give Piet some sugar and yeast and things from the stores, for them to make beer tomorrow when he was gone. He put his hands deep in his pockets and stretched out to the fire with his head sunk on his chest. The lyre-player picked up his flimsy piece of wood again, and slowly what the young man was feeling inside himself seemed to find a voice; up into the night beyond the fire, it went, uncoiling [1] from his breast and bringing ease. As if it had been made audible out of infinity and could be returned to infinity at any point, the lonely voice of the lyre went on and on. Nobody spoke, the barriers of tongues fell with silence. The whole dirty tide of worry and planning had gone out of the young man. The small, high moon, outshone by a spiky spread of cold stars, repeated the shape of the lyre. He sat for he was not aware how long, just as he had for so many other nights, with the stars at his head and the fire at his feet.

But at last the music stopped and time began again. There was tonight; there was tomorrow, when he was going to drive to Francistown. He stood up; the company fragmented. The lyre-player blew his nose into his fingers. Dusty feet took their accustomed weight. They went off to their tents and he went off to his. Faint plangencies [2] followed them. The young man gave a

1. *uncoiling* : (here) coming out slowly, with a release of tension.
2. *plangencies* : low, sad sounds.

loud, ugly, animal yawn, the sort of unashamed personal noise a man can make when he lives alone. He walked very slowly across the sand; it was dark but he knew the way more surely than with his eyes. 'Piet! Hey!' he bawled [1] as he reached his tent. 'You get up early tomorrow, eh? And I don't want to hear the lorry won't [2] start. You get it going and then you call me. D'you hear?'

He was lighting the oil lamp that Piet had left ready on the chest and as it came up softly it brought the whole interior of the tent with it: the chest, the bed, the clock, and the coy smiling face of the seventeen-year-old girl. He sat down on the bed, sliding his palms through the silky fur of the kaross. He drew a breath and held it for a moment, looking round purposefully. And then he picked up the photograph, folded the cardboard support back flat to the frame, and put it in the chest with all his other things, ready for the journey.

---

1. *bawled* : called loudly.
2. *I don't want to hear the lorry won't start* : you must make sure the lorry is working properly tomorrow morning.

Characters

1. The title of the story draws our attention to one aspect of the protagonist. What other roles does he play? Why has the author chosen to emphasise his role as a bridegroom? Does he seem to be very deeply in love?

2. Which of the adjectives listed below best describes Piet's attitude to the young man?

> affectionate   aggressive   deferential
>   disrespectful   indifferent   intimate

(You may choose more than one.)

3. What emotion is suggested by the young man's feeling hot after he promises to bring a radio for his black colleagues (p. 17)?

Setting

1. Read the first three paragraphs of the story again. How does the description in paragraph 3 differ from the first two paragraphs?

2. What do you think koeksusters are? Great importance is given to them in the story: why? What is suggested about the young man through the koeksusters?

Structure

Nothing important happens in the course of the story, yet there is a clear development from the young man's arrival at the camp to the moment when he packs the photograph of his bride. What are the stages of this development?

Symbolism

1. Can the photograph of the seventeen-year-old girl be seen as a symbol? Of what?

2. Explain the significance of the music played by the black men and the young man's promise to bring them 'real music' through the radio.

Language

1. Onomatopoeia is the use of words which sound like the noise they refer to (such as bang, crack, hiss). Find at least five examples of onomatopoeia in the story. Can you suggest why this device is used so frequently here?

2. From the context, work out the probable meaning of:

   i. kaross
   ii. Ou Piet, ek wag
   iii. baas
   iv. Kèrel!

3. Look at the dialogue between the young man and Piet. What grammatical characteristics differentiate it from the rest of the story? Why should this be the case?

4. What does Gordimer mean when she writes that the black men by the fire were 'painted by it' (p. 16)?

Narrator

1. Which of the following is the most accurate description of this story?

    i. It is told entirely through the young man's thoughts.

    ii. The author intervenes in the young man's thoughts at some points.

    Quote from the text to support your answer.

2. We never learn the young man's name. How does this affect our attitude to him?

3. How does the narrator suggest the sense of a familiar routine? Use quotations from the story in your answer.

Themes

1. Is the marriage between the young man and the 17-year-old girl likely to be a happy one? Explain the reasons for your answer.

2. Black and white, in this story, live separately within the same community. When the story was written, apartheid – the obligatory separation of people of different races – was still in force in South Africa. What do you think of apartheid? Does Nadine Gordimer show what she thinks of it in the story? Do the black people in the story seem to be suffering under this system?

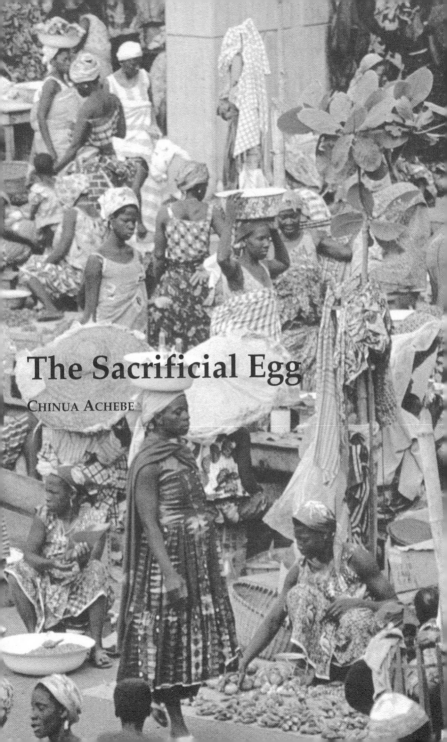

The Sacrificial Egg

Chinua Achebe

Chinua Achebe 1930-

Educated in his native Nigeria at a primary school run by missionaries (his father was a catechist for the Church Mission Society), at the prestigious Government College in Umuahia and at University College, Ibadan (a constituent college of the University of London), Achebe originally wanted to become a doctor, but ultimately chose to study English Literature, graduating in 1953. For many years he worked for the Nigerian Broadcasting Corporation, but during the Nigerian Civil War (1967-70) he went on missions to other countries in support of Biafra. After the war he became a university teacher in Nigeria, Canada and the USA. His novels cover one hundred years of Nigerian history and clearly show his understanding of the tensions in African society between the traditional and the modern, the individual and the community. He is one of the best-known African writers, whose work has been translated into many languages. Despite his largely 'English' education, he has never forgotten his African heritage and has tried to use his literary gifts in the service of his society.

JULIUS OBI SAT GAZING AT HIS TYPEWRITER. The fat chief clerk, his boss, was snoring at his table. Outside, the gatekeeper in his green uniform was sleeping at his post. No customer had passed through the gate for nearly a week. There was an empty basket on the giant weighing machine. A few palm kernels lay in the dust around the machine.

Julius went to the window that overlooked the great market on the banks of the Niger. This market, like all Ibo [1] markets, had been held on one of the four days of the week. But with the coming of the white man and the growth of Umuru into a big palm-oil port, it had become a daily market. In spite of that, however, it was still busiest on its original Nkwo day, because the deity that presided over it cast her spell only on that day. It was said that she appeared in the form of an old woman in the centre of the market just before cockcrow [2] and waved her magic fan in the four directions of the earth – in front of her, behind her, to the right, and to the left – to draw to the market men and women from distant clans. And they came, these men and women, bringing the produce of their lands: palm-oil and kernels, kola nuts, cassava, [3] mats, baskets, and earthenware pots. And they took home many-coloured cloths, smoked fish, iron pots and plates.

1. *Ibo* ['iːbəʊ] : a Nigerian tribe.
2. *cockcrow* : sunrise (the time when cocks begin to crow).
3. *cassava* : plant with thick roots, grown for food.

Others came by the great river bringing yams [1] and fish in their canoes. Sometimes it was a big canoe with a dozen or more people in it; sometimes it was just a fisherman and his wife in a small vessel from the swift-flowing Anambara. They moored their canoe on the bank and sold their fish, after much haggling. The woman then walked up the steep banks of the river to the heart of the market to buy salt and oil and, if the sales had been good, a length of cloth. And for her children at home she bought bean cakes or *akara* and *maimai*, which the Igara women cooked. As evening approached, they took up their paddles and paddled away, the water shimmering in the sunset and their canoe becoming smaller and smaller in the distance until it was just a dark crescent on the water's face and two dark bodies swaying forwards and backwards in it.

Julius Obi was not a native of Umuru. He came from a bush [2] village twenty or so miles away. But having passed his Standard Six [3] in a mission school [4] in 1920 he came to Umuru to work as a clerk in the offices of the Niger Company, which dealt in palm-oil and kernels. The offices were situated beside the famous Umuru market, so that in his first two or three weeks Julius had to learn to work against the background of its noise. Sometimes when the chief clerk was away or asleep he walked to the window and looked down on the vast anthill [5] activity. Most of these people were not there yesterday, he thought, and yet the market was as full. There must be many, many people in the world. Of course they say that not everyone who came to the great market was a real person. Janet's mother had said so.

---

1. *yams* : root vegetables, rather like potatoes.
2. *bush* : (Africa) remote country area covered with natural bushes and trees.
3. *Standard Six* : the top level of compulsory education.
4. *mission school* : school for native children run by European missionaries.
5. *anthill* : mound of earth made by ants; used here because the people in the market seem to be as numerous and busy as ants.

'Some of the beautiful young women you see squeezing through the crowds are not real people but *mammy-wota* from the river,' she said.

'How does one know them?' asked Julius, whose education placed him above such superstitious stuff. But he took care not to sound unbelieving. He had long learned that it was bad policy to argue with Ma on such points.

'You can always tell,' she explained, 'because they are beautiful with a beauty that is not of this world. You catch a glimpse of them with the tail of your eye, then they disappear in the crowd.'

Julius thought about these things as he now stood at the window looking down at the empty market. Who would have believed that the great market could ever be so empty? But such was the power of *Kitikpa*, or smallpox.

When Umuru had been a little village, it had been swept and kept clean by its handful of inhabitants. But now it had grown into a busy, sprawling, [1] crowded, and dirty river port. And *Kitikpa* came. No other disease is feared by the Ibo people as much as they fear *Kitikpa*. It is personified as an evil deity. Its victims are not mourned lest it be offended. It put an end to the coming and going between neighbours and between villages. They said, '*Kitikpa* is in that village,' and immediately it was cut off by its neighbours.

Julius was worried because it was almost a week since he had seen Janet, the girl he was going to marry. Ma had explained to him very gently that he should no longer come to see them 'until this thing is over by the power of Jehovah'. Ma was a very devout Christian, and one reason why she approved of Julius for her only daughter was that he sang in the church choir.

'You must keep to your rooms,' she had said. 'You never know whom you might meet on the streets. That family has got it.' She pointed at the house across the road. 'That is what the yellow palm frond at the doorway means. The family were all moved away today in the big government lorry.'

---

1. *sprawling* : covering a large area (often used of towns which have grown rapidly).

Janet walked a short way with him, and they said good night. And they shook hands, which was very odd.

Julius did not go straight home. He went to the bank of the river and just walked up and down it. He must have been there a long time, because he was still there when the *ekwe*, or wooden gong, of the night spirit sounded. He immediately set out for home, half walking and half running. He had about half an hour to get home before the spirit ran its race through the town.

As Julius hurried home he stepped on something that broke with a slight liquid explosion. He stopped and peeped down at the footpath. The moon was not yet up, but there was some faint light which showed that it would not be long delayed. In this light Julius saw that he had stepped on a sacrificial egg. There were young palm fronds around it. Someone oppressed by misfortune had brought the offering to the crossroads in the dusk. And he had stepped on it, and taken the sufferer's ill luck to himself. 'Nonsense,' he said and hurried away. But it was too late; the night spirit was already abroad. Its voice rose high and clear in the still, black air. It was a long way away, but Julius knew that distance did not apply to these beings. So he made straight for the cocoyam [1] farm beside the road and threw himself on his belly. He had hardly done this when he heard the rattling staff [2] of the spirit and a thundering stream of esoteric speech. He shook all over. The sounds came bearing down on him. And then he could hear the footsteps. It was as if twenty men were running together. In no time at all the sounds had passed and disappeared in the distance on the other side of the road.

As Julius stood at the window looking out on the empty market he lived through that night again. It was only a week ago, but already it seemed to be separated from the present by a vast emptiness. This emptiness deepened with the passage of time. On this side stood Julius, and on the other Ma and Janet, who were carried away by the smallpox.

1. *cocoyam* : West African plant grown for food.
2. *staff* : strong wooden stick.

Characters

1. Achebe writes that Julius's 'education placed him above such superstitious stuff'. Find evidence in the story both for and against this statement.

2. 'Ma was a very devout Christian.' What is surprising about this statement?

Setting

1. How does Achebe represent the unresolved tension between the modern world and African traditions through the setting of this story?

2. Make a list of objects mentioned in the story which evoke the African background.

Structure

We learn Ma's and Janet's destiny only in the last sentence of the story. How is it anticipated elsewhere?

Symbolism

1. In addition to its function in the development of the story, can the egg be said to symbolise something or someone?

2. Why should an egg be chosen as a sacrificial object?

Language

1. What is suggested by 'anthill activity' (p. 26)?

2. How would you translate *mammy-wota*, judging from the context?

3. Why is there a change of tense from past to present in the paragraph beginning 'When Umuru had been a little village' (p. 27)?

4. What does Julius mean when he says 'Nonsense' to himself?

Narrator

Which is the most accurate description of this story?

i. It is told by an omniscient narrator.

ii. It is told in the third person from one character's point of view.

iii. It is told in the first person.

Themes

1. Does Achebe treat superstition seriously in the story? Do you agree with his attitude?

2. The concept of 'emptiness' is used in two different senses in the last paragraph. What are they? Do you find them effective? How are they connected?

Minutes Of Glory

NGUGI WA THIONG'O

Ngugi wa Thiong'o 1938-

A graduate of Makerere University College, Kenya, James Ngugi – as he was originally called – has written in both English and his first language, Kikuyu. His first Kikuyu novel was largely written in prison, where he was confined without trial from 1977 to 1978 as a result of Kenya's censorship laws, and a number of his works – he is both a novelist and a playwright – have been banned in his native country. He has been supported by Writers and Scholars International, an association dedicated to promoting intellectual and artistic freedom. It is characteristic of his writing, as in *Minutes Of Glory*, that a realistic account of Kenyan life should be leavened with compassion. Ngugi wa Thiong'o now writes exclusively in Kikuyu or Kiswahili, although he still uses English to translate his works and especially for political purposes. He is an active supporter of African oral traditions and tribal values against the imported values of colonialism.

HER NAME WAS WANJIRU. But she liked better her Christian one, Beatrice. It sounded more pure and more beautiful. Not that she was ugly; but she could not be called beautiful either. Her body, dark and full fleshed, had the form, yes, but it was as if it waited to be filled by the spirit. She worked in beer-halls where sons of women came to drown their inner lives in beer cans and froth. Nobody seemed to notice her. Except, perhaps, when a proprietor or an impatient customer called out her name, Beatrice; then other customers would raise their heads briefly, a few seconds, as if to behold the bearer of such a beautiful name, but not finding anybody there, they would resume their drinking, their ribald jokes, their laughter and play with the other serving girls. She was like a wounded bird in flight: a forced landing now and then but nevertheless wobbling from place to place so that she would variously be found in Alaska, Paradise, The Modern, Thome and other beer-halls all over Limuru. Sometimes it was because an irate proprietor found she was not attracting enough customers; he would sack [1] her without notice and without a salary. She would wobble to the next bar. But sometimes she was simply tired of nesting in one place, a daily witness of familiar scenes; girls even more decidedly ugly than she were fought over by numerous

1. *sack* : dismiss.

claimants at closing hours. What do they have that I don't have? she would ask herself, depressed. She longed for a bar-kingdom where she would be at least one of the rulers, where petitioners would bring their gifts of beer, frustrated smiles and often curses that hid more lust and love than hate.

She left Limuru town proper and tried the mushrooming townlets [1] around. She worked at Ngarariga, Kamiritho, Rironi and even Tiekunu and everywhere the story was the same. Oh, yes, occasionally she would get a client; but none cared for her as she would have liked, none really wanted her enough to fight over her. She was always a hard-up [2] customer's last resort. [3] No make-believe even, not for her that sweet pretence that men indulged in after their fifth bottle of Tusker. The following night or during a pay-day, the same client would pretend not to know her; he would be trying his money-power over girls who already had more than a fair share of admirers.

She resented this. She saw in every girl a rival and adopted a sullen attitude. Nyagūthiī especially was the thorn that always pricked her wounded flesh. [4] Nyagūthiī arrogant and aloof, but men always in her courtyard; Nyagūthiī fighting with men, and to her they would bring propitiating gifts which she accepted as of right. [5] Nyagūthiī could look bored, impatient, or downright [6] contemptuous and still men would cling to her as if they enjoyed being whipped with biting words, curled lips and the indifferent eyes of a free woman. Nyagūthiī was also a bird in flight, never really able to settle in one place, but in her case it

---

1. *mushrooming townlets* : little towns which had grown very quickly, like mushrooms.
2. *hard-up* : having little money.
3. *last resort* : solution if everything else fails.
4. *the thorn that always pricked her wounded flesh* : this is a variation on the common expression a thorn in one's flesh, which means a cause of continual pain or suffering.
5. *as of right* : as something she had a right to.
6. *downright* : completely.

was because she hungered for change and excitement: new faces and new territories for her conquest. Beatrice resented her very shadow. She saw in her the girl she would have liked to be, a girl who was both totally immersed in and yet completely above the underworld of bar violence and sex. Wherever Beatrice went the long shadow of Nyagūthiī would sooner or later follow her.

She fled Limuru for Ilmorog in Chiri District. Ilmorog had once been a ghost village, but had been resurrected to life by that legendary woman, Nyang'endo, to whom every pop group had paid their tribute. It was of her that the young dancing Muthuu and Muchun g'wa sang:

> When I left Nairobi for Ilmorog
> Never did I know
> I would bear this wonder-child mine
> Nyang'endo.

As a result, Ilmorog was always seen as a town of hope where the weary and the down-trodden [1] would find their rest and fresh water. But again Nyagūthiī followed her.

She found that Ilmorog, despite the legend, despite the songs and dances, was not different from Limuru. She tried various tricks. Clothes? But even here she never earned enough to buy herself glittering robes. What was seventy-five shillings a month without house allowance, posho, [2] without salaried boy-friends? By that time, Ambi [3] had reached Ilmorog, and Beatrice thought that this would be the answer. Had she not, in Limuru, seen girls blacker than herself transformed overnight from ugly sins into white stars by a touch of skinlightening creams? And men would ogle [4] them, would even talk with exaggerated pride of

---

1. *down-trodden* : treated without respect.
2. *posho* : (Swahili) daily rations.
3. *Ambi* : skin-lightening product.
4. *ogle* ['əʊgəl] : look at with sexual interest.

their newborn girl friends. Men were strange creatures, Beatrice thought in moments of searching analysis. They talked heatedly against Ambi, Butone, Firesnow, Moonsnow,[1] wigs, straightened hair; but they always went for a girl with an Ambi-lightened skin and head covered with a wig made in imitation of European or Indian hair. Beatrice never tried to find the root cause of this black self-hatred, she simply accepted the contradiction and applied herself to Ambi with a vengeance.[2] She had to rub out her black shame. But even Ambi she could not afford in abundance; she could only apply it to her face and her arms so that her legs and neck retained their blackness. Besides there were parts of her face she could not readily reach – behind the ears and above the eyelashes, for instance – and these were a constant source of shame and irritation for her Ambi-self.

She would always remember this Ambi period as one of her deepest humiliation before her later minutes of glory. She worked in Ilmorog Starlight Bar and Lodging. Nyagūthiī with her bangled[3] hands, her huge earrings, served behind the counter. The owner was a good Christian soul who regularly went to church and paid all his dues to Harambee[4] projects. Pot-belly.[5] Grey hairs. Soft-spoken. A respectable family man, well known in Ilmorog. Hardworking even, for he would not leave the bar until the closing hours, or more precisely, until Nyagūthiī left. He had no eyes for any other girl; he hung around her, and surreptitiously brought her gifts of clothes without receiving gratitude in kind. Only the promise. Only the hope for tomorrow. Other girls he gave eighty shillings a month. Nyagūthiī had a room to herself. Nyagūthiī woke up whenever

1. *Butone, Firesnow, Moonsnow* : skin-lightening products.
2. *with a vengeance* : with great energy.
3. *bangled* : decorated with rings on the wrists.
4. *Harambee* : co-operative set up by the Kenyan government for schooling.
5. *Potbelly* : protruding stomach.

she liked to take the stock. But Beatrice and the other girls had to wake up at five or so, make tea for the lodgers, clean up the bar and wash dishes and glasses. Then they would hang around the bar and in shifts [1] until two o'clock when they would go for a small break. At five o'clock, they had to be in again, ready for customers whom they would now serve with frothy beers and smiles until twelve o'clock or for as long as there were customers thirsty for more Tuskers and Pilsners. [2] What often galled [3] Beatrice, although in her case it did not matter one way or another, was the owner's insistence that the girls should sleep in Starlight. They would otherwise be late for work, he said. But what he really wanted was for the girls to use their bodies to attract more lodgers in Starlight. Most of the girls, led by Nyagũthiĩ defied the rule and bribed the watchman to let them out and in. They wanted to meet their regular or one-night boy-friends in places where they would be free and where they would be treated as not just barmaids. Beatrice always slept in. Her occasional one-night patrons wanted to spend the minimum. Came a night when the owner, refused by Nyagũthiĩ, approached her. He started by finding fault with her work; he called her names, then as suddenly he started praising her, although in a grudging almost contemptuous manner. He grabbed her, struggled with her, pot-belly, grey hairs, and everything. Beatrice felt an unusual revulsion for the man. She could not, she would not bring herself to accept that which had so recently been cast aside by Nyagũthiĩ. My God, she wept inside, what does Nyagũthiĩ have that I don't have? The man now humiliated himself before her. He implored. He promised her gifts. But she would not yield. That night she too defied the rule. She jumped through a window; she sought a bed in another bar and only came back at six. The proprietor called her

---

1. *shifts* : different periods of work.
2. *Tuskers and Pilsners* : kinds of beer.
3. *galled* [gɔːld] : irritated.

in front of all the others and dismissed her. But Beatrice was rather surprised at herself.

She stayed a month without a job. She lived from room to room at the capricious mercy of the other girls. [1] She did not have the heart to leave Ilmorog and start all over again in a new town. The wound hurt. She was tired of wandering. She stopped using Ambi. No money. She looked at herself in the mirror. She had so aged, hardly a year after she had fallen from grace. Why then was she scrupulous, she would ask herself. But somehow she had a horror of soliciting [2] lovers or directly bartering [3] her body for hard cash. [4] What she wanted was decent work and a man or several men who cared for her. Perhaps she took that need for a man, for a home and for a child with her to bed. Perhaps it was this genuine need that scared off men who wanted other things from barmaids. She wept late at nights and remembered home. At such moments, her mother's village in Nyeri seemed the sweetest place on God's earth. She would invest the life of her peasant mother and father with romantic illusions of immeasurable peace and harmony. She longed to go back home to see them. But how could she go back with empty hands? In any case the place was now a distant landscape in the memory. Her life was here in the bar among this crowd of lost strangers. Fallen from grace, fallen from grace. She was part of a generation which would never again be one with the soil, the crops, the wind and the moon. Not for them that whispering in dark hedges, not for her that dance and love-making under the glare of the moon, with the hills of Tumu Tumu rising to touch the sky. She remembered that girl from her home village who, despite a life of apparent glamour being the kept mistress [5] of

1. *at the capricious mercy of the other girls* : depending on the other girls' changing ideas.
2. *soliciting* : offering herself for sex.
3. *bartering* : exchanging for money.
4. *hard cash* : notes and coins.
5. *kept mistress* : woman who is financially supported in return for sex.

one rich man after another in Limuru, had gassed herself to death. This generation was now awed by the mystery of death, just as it was callous [1] to the mystery of life; for how many unmarried mothers had thrown their babies into latrines [2] rather than lose that glamour? The girl's death became the subject of jokes. She had gone metric – without pains, they said. Thereafter, for a week, Beatrice thought of going metric. But she could not bring herself to do it.

She wanted love; she wanted life.

A new bar was opened in Ilmorog. Treetop Bar, Lodging and Restaurant. Why Treetop, Beatrice could not understand unless because it was a storied [3] building: tea-shop on the ground floor and beer-shop in a room at the top. The rest were rooms for five-minute or one-night lodgers. The owner was a retired civil servant but one who still played at politics. He was enormously wealthy with business sites and enterprises in every major town in Kenya. Big shots [4] from all over the country came to his bar. Big men in Mercedes. Big men in their Bentleys. Big men in their Jaguars and Daimlers. Big men with uniformed chauffeurs drowsing with boredom in cars waiting outside. There were others not so big who came to pay respects to the great. They talked politics mostly. And about their work. Gossip was rife. [5] Didn't you know? Indeed so and so has been promoted. Really? And so and so has been sacked. Embezzlement [6] of public funds. So foolish you know. Not clever about it at all. They argued, they quarrelled, sometimes they fought it out with fists, especially during the elections campaign. The only point on which they were all agreed was that the Luo [7] community was

1. *callous* : totally insensitive.
2. *latrines* [lə'triːns] : toilets.
3. *storied* : on several floors.
4. *Big shots* : important people.
5. *rife* : widespread.
6. *Embezzlement* : stealing from one's place of work.
7. *Luo* : an East African tribe.

the root cause of all the trouble in Kenya; that intellectuals and University students were living in an ivory tower [1] of privilege and arrogance; that Kiambu had more than a lion's share of developments; that men from Nyeri and Muranga had acquired all the big business in Nairobi and were even encroaching on Chiri District; that African workers, especially those on the farms, were lazy and jealous of 'us' who had sweated ourselves to sudden prosperity. Otherwise each would hymn his own praises or return compliments. Occasionally in moments of drunken ebullience and self-praise, one would order two rounds of beer [2] for each man present in the bar. Even the poor from Ilmorog would come to Treetop to dine at the gates of the nouveaux riches. [3]

Here Beatrice got a job as a sweeper and bedmaker. Here for a few weeks she felt closer to greatness. Now she made beds for men she had previously known as names. She watched how even the poor tried to drink and act big in front of the big. But soon fate caught up with her. Girls flocked to Treetop from other bars. Girls she had known at Limuru, girls she had known at Ilmorog. And most had attached themselves to one or several big men, often playing a hide-and-not-to-be-found [4] game with their numerous lovers. And Nyagūthiī was there behind the counter, with the eyes of the rich and the poor fixed on her. And she, with her big eyes, bangled hands and earrings maintained the same air of bored indifference. Beatrice as a sweeper and bedmaker became even more invisible. Girls who had fallen into good fortune looked down upon her.

She fought life with dreams. In between putting clean sheets on beds that had just witnessed a five-minute struggle that

1. *ivory tower* : imaginary ideal place, especially for intellectuals.
2. *rounds of beer* : drinks bought for everyone present.
3. *nouveaux riches* [nuːvəʊ 'riːʃ] : (French) people who have recently made a lot of money.
4. *hide-and-not-to-be-found* : more usually *hide and seek*, children's game in which somebody hides and the others look for her/him.

ended in a half-strangled cry and a pool, [1] she would stand by
the window and watch the cars and the chauffeurs, so that soon
she knew all the owners by the number plates of their cars and
the uniforms of their chauffeurs. She dreamt of lovers who
would come for her in sleek [2] Mercedes sports cars made for
two. She saw herself linking hands with such a lover, walking in
the streets of Nairobi and Mombasa, tapping the ground with
high heels, quick, quick short steps. And suddenly she would
stop in front of a display glass window, exclaiming at the same
time, Oh darling, won't you buy me those . . . ? Those what? he
would ask, affecting anger. Those stockings, darling. It was as
an owner of several stockings, ladderless [3] and holeless, that she
thought of her well-being. Never again would she mend torn
things. Never, never, never. Do you understand? Never. She
was next the proud owner of different coloured wigs, blonde
wigs, brunette wigs, redhead wigs, Afro wigs, wigs, wigs, all the
wigs in the world. Only then would the whole earth sing
hallelujah to the one Beatrice. At such moments, she would feel
exalted, lifted out of her murky [4] self, no longer a floor sweeper
and bedmaker for a five-minute instant love, but Beatrice,
descendant of Wangu Makeri who made men tremble with
desire at her naked body bathed in moonlight, daughter of
Nyang'endo, the founder of modern Ilmorog, of whom they
often sang that she had worked several lovers into impotence.

Then she noticed him and he was the opposite of the lover of
her dreams. He came one Saturday afternoon driving a big five-
ton lorry. He carefully parked it beside the Benzes, the Jaguars
and the Daimlers, not as a lorry, but as one of those sleek cream-
bodied frames, so proud of it he seemed to be. He dressed in a
baggy grey suit over which he wore a heavy khaki military
overcoat. He removed the overcoat, folded it with care, and put

---

1. *pool* : (here) semen spilled on the sheets during the sex act.
2. *sleek* : (here) shiny and elegant.
3. *ladderless* : undamaged (of stockings or tights).
4. *murky* ['mɔːki] : dark and unpleasant.

it in the front seat. He locked all the doors, dusted himself a little, then walked round the lorry as if inspecting it for damage. A few steps before he entered Treetop, he turned round for a final glance at his lorry dwarfing the other things. At Treetops he sat in a corner and, with a rather loud defiant voice, ordered a Kenya one. [1] He drank it with relish, looking around at the same time for a face he might recognize. He indeed did recognize one of the big ones and he immediately ordered for him a quarter bottle of Vat 69. [2] This was accepted with a bare nod of the head and a patronising smile; but when he tried to follow his generosity with a conversation, he was firmly ignored. He froze, [3] sank into his Muratina. [4] But only for a time. He tried again: he was met with frowning faces. More pathetic were his attempts to join in jokes; he would laugh rather too loudly, which would make the big ones stop, leaving him in the air alone. Later in the evening he stood up, counted several crisp hundred shilling notes and handed them to Nyagūthiī behind the counter ostensibly for safekeeping. People whispered; murmured; a few laughed, rather derisively, though they were rather impressed. But this act did not win him immediate recognition. He staggered towards room no. 7 which he had hired. Beatrice brought him the keys. He glanced at her, briefly, then lost all interest.

Thereafter he came every Saturday. At five when most of the big shots were already seated. He repeated the same ritual, except the money act, and always met with defeat. He nearly always sat in the same corner and always rented room 7. Beatrice grew to anticipate his visits and, without being conscious of it, kept the room ready for him. Often after he had been badly humiliated by the big company, he would detain

1. *Kenya one* : a local brand of beer.
2. *Vat 69* : a cheap brand of whisky.
3. *froze* : (here) stopped moving completely.
4. *Muratina* : kind of beer.

Beatrice and talk to her, or rather he talked to himself in her presence. For him, it had been a life of struggles. He had never been to school although getting an education had been his ambition. He never had a chance. His father was a squatter [1] in the European settled area in the Rift Valley. [2] That meant a lot in those colonial days. It meant among other things a man and his children were doomed to a future of sweat and toil for the white devils and their children. He had joined the freedom struggle and like the others had been sent to detention. He came from detention the same as his mother had brought him to this world. Nothing. With independence he found he did not possess the kind of education which would have placed him in one of the vacancies at the top. He started as a charcoal burner, then a butcher, gradually working his own way to become a big transporter of vegetables and potatoes from the Rift Valley and Chiri districts to Nairobi. He was proud of his achievement. But he resented that others, who had climbed to their present wealth through loans and a subsidized education, would not recognize his like. [3] He would rumble on [4] like this, dwelling on education he would never have, and talking of better chances for his children. Then he would carefully count the money, put it under the pillow, and then dismiss Beatrice. Occasionally he would buy her a beer but he was clearly suspicious of women whom he saw as money-eaters of men. He had not yet married.

One night he slept with her. In the morning he scratched [5] for a twenty shilling note and gave it to her. She accepted the money with an odd feeling of guilt. He did this for several weeks. She did not mind the money. It was useful. But he paid for her body as he would pay for a bag of potatoes or a sack of

---

1. *squatter* : someone living on someone else's land without permission and without paying rent.
2. *Rift Valley* : a valley in East Africa, on the borders of Uganda.
3. *his like* : people like him.
4. *rumble on* : talk at length in a deep voice.
5. *scratched* : looked around anxiously.

cabbages. With the one pound, he had paid for her services as a listener, a vessel of his complaints against those above, and as a one-night receptacle of his man's burden. She was becoming bored with his ego, with his stories that never varied in content, but somehow, in him, deep inside, she felt that something had been there, a fire, a seed, a flower which was being smothered. In him she saw a fellow victim and looked forward to his visits. She too longed to talk to someone. She too longed to confide in a human being who would understand.

And she did it one Saturday night, suddenly interrupting the story of his difficult climb to the top. She did not know why she did it. Maybe it was the rain outside. It was softly drumming the corrugated iron sheets, [1] bringing with the drumming a warm and drowsy indifference. He would listen. He had to listen. She came from Karatina in Nyeri. Her two brothers had been gunned down [2] by the British soldiers. Another one had died in detention. She was, so to speak, an only child. Her parents were poor. But they worked hard on their bare strip of land and managed to pay her fees in primary school. For the first six years she had worked hard. In the seventh year, she must have relaxed a little. She did not pass with a good grade. Of course she knew many with similar grades who had been called to good government secondary schools. She knew a few others with lesser grades who had gone to very top schools on the strength of their connections. But she was not called to any high school with reasonable fees. Her parents could not afford fees in a Harambee school. And she would not hear of repeating standard seven. She stayed at home with her parents. Occasionally she would help them in the shamba [3] and with house chores. But imagine: for the past six years she had led a life with a different rhythm from that of her parents. Life in the

---

1. *corrugated iron sheets* : large pieces of metal in wave-like folds, used as a roof.
2. *gunned down* : killed with guns.
3. *shamba* : (Swahili) small farm.

'Life in the village was dull.'

village was dull. She would often go to Karatina and to Nyeri in search of work. In every office, they would ask her the same questions: what work do you want? What do you know? Can you type? Can you take shorthand? [1] She was desperate. It was in Nyeri, drinking Fanta in a shop, tears in her eyes, that she met a young man in a dark suit and sun-glasses. He saw her plight and talked to her. He came from Nairobi. Looking for work? That's easy, in a big city there would be no difficulty with jobs. He would certainly help. Transport? He had a car – a cream-white Peugeot. Heaven. It was a beautiful ride, with the promise of dawn. Nairobi. He drove her to Terrace Bar. They drank beer and talked about Nairobi. Through the window she could see the neon-lit city and knew that here was hope. That night she gave herself to him, with the promise of dawn making her feel

---

1. *take shorthand* : use a system of fast writing to take dictation.

light and gay. She had a very deep sleep. When she woke in the morning, the man in the cream-white Peugeot was not there. She never saw him again. That's how she had started the life of a barmaid. And for one and a half years now she had not been once to see her parents. Beatrice started weeping. Huge sobs of self-pity. Her humiliation and constant flight were fresh in her mind. She had never been able to take to bar culture, she always thought that something better would come her way. But she was trapped, it was the only life she now knew, although she had never really learnt all its laws and norms. Again she heaved out and in,[1] tears tossing out with every sob. Then suddenly she froze. Her sobbing was arrested in the air. The man had long covered himself. His snores were huge and unmistakable.

She felt a strange hollowness. Then a bile[2] of bitterness spilt inside her. She wanted to cry at her new failure. She had met several men who had treated her cruelly, who had laughed at her scruples, at what they thought was an ill-disguised attempt at innocence. She had accepted. But not this, Lord, not this. Was this man not a fellow victim? Had he not, Saturday after Saturday, unburdened himself[3] to her? He had paid for her human services; he had paid away his responsibility with his bottle of Tuskers and hard cash in the morning. Her innermost turmoil had been his lullaby. And suddenly something in her snapped. All the anger of a year and a half, all the bitterness against her humiliation were now directed at this man.

What she did later had the mechanical precision of an experienced hand.

She touched his eyes. He was sound asleep. She raised his head. She let it fall. Her tearless eyes were now cold and set. She removed the pillow from under him. She rummaged through it. She took out his money. She counted five crisp pink notes. She put the money inside her brassiere.

---

1. *heaved out and in* : her chest moved violently because she was crying.
2. *bile* : bitter liquid (here figurative).
3. *unburdened himself* : told her everything.

She went out of room no. 7. Outside it was still raining. She did not want to go to her usual place. She could not now stand the tiny cupboard room or the superior chatter of her roommate. She walked through mud and rain. She found herself walking towards Nyagūthiī's room. She knocked at the door. At first she had no response. Then she heard Nyagūthiī's sleepy voice above the drumming rain.

'Who is that?'

'It is me. Please open.'

'Who?'

'Beatrice.'

'At this hour of the night?'

'Please.'

Lights were put on. Bolts unfastened. The door opened. Beatrice stepped inside. She and Nyagūthiī stood there face to face. Nyagūthiī was in a see-through nightdress: on her shoulders she had a green pullover.

'Beatrice, is there anything wrong?' She at last asked, a note of concern in her voice.

'Can I rest here for a while? I am tired. And I want to talk to you.' Beatrice's voice carried assurance and power.

'But what has happened?'

'I only want to ask you a question, Nyagūthiī'

They were still standing. Then, without a word, they both sat on the bed.

'Why did you leave home, Nyagūthiī?' Beatrice asked. Another silent moment. Nyagūthiī seemed to be thinking about the question. Beatrice waited. Nyagūthiī's voice when at last it came was slightly tremulous, unsteady.

'It is a long story, Beatrice. My father and mother were fairly wealthy. They were also good Christians. We lived under regulations. You must never walk with the heathen. You must not attend their pagan customs – dances and circumcision rites, for instance. There were rules about what, how and when to eat. You must even walk like a Christian lady. You must never be seen with boys. Rules, rules all the way. One day instead of returning home from school, I and another girl from a similar

home ran away to Eastleigh. I have never been home once this
last four years. That's all.'

Another silence. Then they looked at one another in mutual
recognition.

'One more question, Nyagūthiī. You need not answer it. But I
have always thought that you hated me, you despised me.'

'No, no, Beatrice, I have never hated you. I have never hated
anybody. It is just that nothing interests me. Even men do not
move me now. Yet I want, I need instant excitement. I need the
attention of those false flattering eyes to make me feel myself,
myself. But you, you seemed above all this – somehow you had
something inside you that I did not have.'

Beatrice tried to hold her tears with difficulty.

Early the next day, she boarded a bus bound for Nairobi. She
walked down Bazaar Street looking at the shops. Then down
Government Road, right into Kenyatta Avenue, and Kimathi
Street. She went into a shop near Hussein Suleman's Street and
bought several stockings. She put on a pair. She next bought
herself a new dress. Again she changed into it. In a Bata
Shoeshop, she bought high heeled shoes, put them on and
discarded her old flat ones. On to an Akamba kiosk, and she
fitted herself with earrings. She went to a mirror and looked at
her new self. Suddenly she felt enormous hunger as if she had
been hungry all her life. She hesitated in front of Moti Mahal.
Then she walked on, eventually entering Fransae. There was a
glint in her eyes that made men's eyes turn to her. This thrilled
her. She chose a table in a corner and ordered Indian curry. A
man left his table and joined her. She looked at him. Her eyes
were merry. He was dressed in a dark suit and his eyes spoke of
lust. He bought her a drink. He tried to engage her in
conversation. But she ate in silence. He put his hand under the
table and felt her knees. She let him do it. The hand went up and
up her thigh. Then suddenly she left her unfinished food and
her untouched drink and walked out. She felt good. He followed
her. She knew this without once turning her eyes. He walked
beside her for a few yards. She smiled at herself but did not look
at him. He lost his confidence. She left him standing

sheepishly [1] looking at a glass window outside Gino's. In the bus back to Ilmorog, men gave her seats. She accepted this as of right. At Treetops bar she went straight to the counter. The usual crowd of big men were there. Their conversations stopped for a few seconds at her entry. Their lascivious eyes were turned to her. The girls stared at her. Even Nyagūthiī could not maintain her bored indifference. Beatrice bought them drinks. The manager came to her, rather unsure. He tried a conversation. Why had she left work? Where had she been? Would she like to work in the bar, helping Nyagūthiī behind the counter? Now and then? A barmaid brought her a note. A certain big shot wanted to know if she would join their table. More notes came from different big quarters with the one question; would she be free tonight? A trip to Nairobi even. She did not leave her place at the counter. But she accepted their drinks as of right. She felt a new power, confidence even.

She took out a shilling, put it in the slot and the juke box boomed with the voice of Robinson Mwangi singing *Hūnyū wa Mashambani*. He sang of those despised girls who worked on farms and contrasted them with urban girls. Then she played a Kamaru and a D.K. [2] Men wanted to dance with her. She ignored them, but enjoyed their flutter [3] around her. She twisted her hips to the sound of yet another D.K. Her body was free. She was free. She sucked in the excitement and tension in the air.

Then suddenly at around six, the man with the five-ton lorry stormed into the bar. This time he had on his military overcoat. Behind him was a policeman. He looked around. Everybody's eyes were raised to him. But Beatrice went on swaying her hips. At first he could not recognize Beatrice in the girl celebrating her few minutes of glory by the juke box. Then he shouted in triumph. 'That is the girl! Thief! Thief!'

1. *sheepishly* : in an embarrassed manner.
2. *a Kamaru and a D.K.* : popular African recording artists.
3. *flutter* : excitement.

People melted back to their seats. The policeman went and handcuffed her. She did not resist. Only at the door she turned her head and spat. Then she went out followed by the policeman.

In the bar the stunned [1] silence broke into hilarious laughter when someone made a joke about sweetened robbery without violence. They discussed her. Some said she should have been beaten. Others talked contemptuously about 'these bar girls'. Yet others talked with a concern noticeable in unbelieving shakes of their heads about the rising rate of crime. Shouldn't the Hanging Bill be extended to all thefts of property? And without anybody being aware of it the man with the five-ton lorry had become a hero. They now surrounded him with questions and demanded the whole story. Some even bought him drinks. More remarkable, they listened, their attentive silence punctuated by appreciative laughter. The averted threat to property had temporarily knit them into one family. And the man, accepted for the first time, told the story with relish.

But behind the counter Nyagūthiĩ wept.

---

1. *stunned* : shocked.

Characters

1. Re-read the stories of the lorry-driver and Beatrice on pp. 43-6. What do the two characters have in common?

2. How does your view of Nyagũthiĩ change in the course of the story?

3. Thiong'o writes, at the beginning of the story, that Beatrice's 'body, dark and full fleshed, had the form, yes, but it was as if it waited to be filled by the spirit'. Do you feel that Beatrice finds her 'spirit' through her relationship with the lorry-driver and its consequences? Give reasons for your answer.

Setting

1. In what sense is Ilmorog 'a town of hope'?

2. Most of the action of the story takes place in a bar. How does this differ from a bar in your own country? What is the importance of this setting in the development of Beatrice's personality?

Structure

1. Suggest a reason for the isolation of the sentence 'She wanted love; she wanted life' (p. 39) in a separate paragraph. Find other sentences which are isolated in the same way. Do you think the reason is the same in every case?

2. There is no dialogue in the story until Beatrice goes to talk to Nyagũthiĩ after robbing the lorry-driver. What is the effect of this?

Symbolism

1. Nyagũthiĩ is described as 'the thorn that always pricked her [Beatrice's] wounded flesh'. What does this metaphor tell you about the two women?

2. Three metaphors are used about the lorry-driver: 'a fire, a seed, a flower which was being smothered' (p. 44). Does one of these seem particularly appropriate to you? Which one, and why? What do all three metaphors suggest?

3. Beatrice uses the stolen money first to buy clothes and shoes, and later to buy drinks for the men in the Treetops bar. What different aspects of her personality do these choices represent?

Narrator

The story is told almost entirely from one person's point of view: whose? How does this alter in the last two paragraphs? What is the effect of this change of focus?

Themes

1. Beatrice wants to change her appearance by wearing wigs and using products to lighten her skin. Many people nowadays turn to artificial aids of this kind, or to surgery, to make themselves look more attractive. What is your attitude to this?

2. Write a short essay on material poverty as a limitation of personal growth.

Australia

The Union Buries Its Dead

HENRY LAWSON

Henry Lawson 1867-1922

After a difficult childhood, marked by quarrels between his parents and by the onset of deafness when he was only nine years old, Lawson became a journalist, whose interest in the lives of poor people, in the cities and in the wild country known in Australia as 'the bush', found full expression in his verse and short stories. He was never very successful outside his native country, but the realism and dry humour of his best writing made him so popular in Australia that on his death he was given a state funeral – the first Australian writer to be honoured in this way. Most of his writing centres on men, and reflects the tendency in Australia to separate the sexes in accordance with stereotyped ideas about their respective roles. Not all his work is equally effective, partly because of a recurrent drinking problem which ultimately compromised his talent. *The Union Buries Its Dead* is an early story, written when he was only 25, and illustrating his characteristic approach: it is set in the hard world of the bushmen, which it portrays with humour and sympathy.

WHILE OUT BOATING one Sunday afternoon on a billabong [1] across the river, we saw a young man on horseback driving some horses along the bank. He said it was a fine day, and asked if the water was deep there. The joker of our party said it was deep enough to drown him, and he laughed and rode farther up. We didn't take much notice of him.

Next day a funeral gathered at a corner pub and asked each other in to have a drink while waiting for the hearse. They passed away some of the time dancing jigs to a piano in the bar parlour. They passed away the rest of the time sky-larking [2] and fighting.

The defunct was a young union labourer, about twenty-five, who had been drowned the previous day while trying to swim some horses across a billabong of the Darling. [3]

He was almost a stranger in town, and the fact of his having been a union man [4] accounted for the funeral. The police found some union papers in his swag, [5] and called at the General

---

1. *billabong* : (Australian aboriginal) a low area of ground where a river used to be, which only fills up with water when the river floods.
2. *sky-larking* : (informal) having fun.
3. *the Darling* : a river in New South Wales.
4. *a union man* : a member of a workers' organisation.
5. *swag* : (Australian slang) possessions carried in a cloth bag.

Labourers' Union Office for information about him. That's how we knew. The secretary had very little information to give. The departed was a 'Roman',[1] and the majority of the town were otherwise – but unionism is stronger than creed. Drink, however, is stronger than unionism; and, when the hearse presently arrived, more than two-thirds of the funeral were unable to follow. They were too drunk.

The procession numbered fifteen, fourteen souls following the broken shell of a soul. Perhaps not one of the fourteen possessed a soul any more than the corpse did – but that doesn't matter.

Four or five of the funeral, who were boarders[2] at the pub, borrowed a trap[3] which the landlord used to carry passengers to and from the railway station. They were strangers to us who were on foot, and we to them. We were all strangers to the corpse.

A horseman, who looked like a drover[4] just returned from a big trip, dropped into our dusty wake and followed us a few hundred yards, dragging his pack-horse behind him, but a friend made wild and demonstrative signals from a hotel verandah – hooking[5] at the air in front with his right hand and jobbing his left thumb[6] over his shoulder in the direction of the bar – so the drover hauled off[7] and didn't catch up to us any more. He was a stranger to the entire show.

We walked in twos. There were three twos. It was very hot and dusty; the heat rushed in fierce dazzling rays across every

1. *'Roman'* : a Roman Catholic.
2. *boarders* : people who live and eat in someone else's home in return for money.
3. *trap* : two-wheeled vehicle pulled by a horse.
4. *drover* : person whose job is to drive sheep.
5. *hooking* : making gestures like a boxer hitting his opponent.
6. *jobbing his left thumb* : indicating direction with repeated movements of his thumb.
7. *hauled off* : left pulling his horse.

iron roof and light-coloured wall that was turned to the sun. One or two pubs closed respectfully until we got past. They closed their bar doors and the patrons went in and out through some side or back entrance for a few minutes. Bushmen [1] seldom grumble at an inconvenience of this sort, when it is caused by a funeral. They have too much respect for the dead.

On the way to the cemetery we passed three shearers [2] sitting on the shady side of a fence. One was drunk – very drunk. The other two covered their right ears with their hats, out of respect for the departed – whoever he might have been – and one of them kicked the drunk and muttered something to him.

He straightened himself up, stared, and reached helplessly for his hat, which he shoved half off [3] and then on again. Then he made a great effort to pull himself together – and succeeded. He stood up, braced [4] his back against the fence, knocked off his hat, and remorsefully placed his foot on it – to keep it off his head till the funeral passed.

A tall, sentimental drover, who walked by my side, cynically quoted Byronic verses [5] suitable to the occasion – to death – and asked with pathetic humour whether we thought the dead man's ticket [6] would be recognized 'over yonder'. [7] It was a GLU [8] ticket, and the general opinion was that it would be recognized.

Presently my friend said:

'You remember when we were in the boat yesterday, we saw

---

1. *bushmen* : (Australian) men who live in wild country areas.
2. *shearers* : people whose job is to cut the wool off sheep.
3. *shoved half off* : pushed partly off his head.
4. *braced* : leaned for support.
5. *Byronic verses* : lines of poetry in a heroic style, like that of Lord Byron, the Romantic poet.
6. *ticket* : union membership card.
7. *over yonder* : in the afterlife.
8. *GLU* : the General Labourers' Union.

a man driving some horses along the bank?'

'Yes.'

He nodded at the hearse and said:

'Well, that's him.'

I thought awhile.

'I didn't take any particular notice of him,' I said. 'He said something, didn't he?'

'Yes; said it was a fine day. You'd have taken more notice if you'd known that he was doomed to die in the hour, and that those were the last words he would say to any man in this world.'

'To be sure,' said a full voice from the rear. 'If ye'd known that, ye'd have prolonged the conversation.'

We plodded on across the railway line and along the hot, dusty road which ran to the cemetery, some of us talking about the accident, and lying about the narrow escapes we had had ourselves. Presently some one said:

'There's the Devil.'

I looked up and saw a priest standing in the shade of the tree by the cemetery gate.

The hearse was drawn up and the tail-boards [1] were opened. The funeral extinguished its right ear with its hat as four men lifted the coffin out and laid it over the grave. The priest – a pale, quiet young fellow – stood under the shade of a sapling which grew at the head of the grave. He took off his hat, dropped it carelessly on the ground, and proceeded to business. I noticed that one or two heathens [2] winced slightly when the holy water was sprinkled on the coffin. The drops quickly evaporated, and the little round black spots they left were soon dusted over; but the spots showed, by contrast, the cheapness and shabbiness of the cloth with which the coffin was covered. It seemed black before; now it looked a dusky grey.

---

1. *tail-boards* : boards at the back of a van or lorry which can be let down for loading and unloading.

2. *heathens* ['hiːðənz] : here, non-Catholics. Holy water is not used by other denominations except for baptisms.

Just here man's ignorance and vanity made a farce of the funeral. A big, bull-necked publican, [1] with heavy, blotchy features, and a supremely ignorant expression, picked up the priest's straw hat and held it about two inches over the head of his reverence during the whole of the service. The father, be it remembered, was standing in the shade. A few shoved their hats on and off uneasily, struggling between their disgust for the living and their respect for the dead. The hat had a conical crown [2] and a brim sloping down all round like a sunshade, and the publican held it with his great red claw spread over the crown. To do the priest justice, perhaps he didn't notice the incident. A stage priest or parson [3] in the same position might have said, 'Put the hat down, my friend; is not the memory of our departed brother worth more than my complexion?' A wattlebark layman [4] might have expressed himself in stronger language, none the less to the point. But my priest seemed unconscious of what was going on. Besides, the publican was a great and important pillar of the Church. [5] He couldn't, as an ignorant and conceited ass, lose such a good opportunity of asserting his faithfulness and importance to his Church.

The grave looked very narrow under the coffin, and I drew a breath of relief when the box slid easily down. I saw a coffin get stuck once, at Rookwood, and it had to be yanked out with difficulty, and laid on the sods at the feet of the heart-broken relations, who howled dismally while the grave-diggers widened the hole. But they don't cut contracts so fine [6] in the

1. *publican* : owner of a pub.
2. *crown* : part of a hat which covers the top of the head.
3. *a stage priest or parson* : a Catholic or Protestant minister in a play performed on the stage.
4. *a wattlebark* ['wɒtəlbɑːk] *layman* : (Australian) a countryman who was not a priest. The wattle is a common Australian tree.
5. *pillar of the Church* : active and important member of the local Church.
6. *they don't cut contracts so fine* : they are not so ungenerous. To 'cut something fine' is to do the minimum necessary.

West. Our grave-digger was not altogether bowelless, [1] and, out of respect for that human quality described as 'feelin's', he scraped up some light and dusty soil and threw it down to deaden the fall of the clay lumps on the coffin. He also tried to steer the first few shovelfuls gently down against the end of the grave with the back of the shovel turned outwards, but the hard, dry Darling River clods rebounded and knocked all the same. It didn't matter much – nothing does. The fall of lumps of clay on a stranger's coffin doesn't sound any different from the fall of the same things on an ordinary wooden box – at least I didn't notice anything awesome or unusual in the sound; but, perhaps, one of us – the most sensitive – might have been impressed by being reminded of a burial of long ago, when the thump of every sod jolted his heart.

I have left out the wattle [2] – because it wasn't there. I have also neglected to mention the heart-broken old mate, with his grizzled [3] head bowed and great pearly drops streaming down his rugged [4] cheeks. He was absent – he was probably 'Out Back'. For similar reasons I have omitted reference to the suspicious moisture [5] in the eyes of a bearded bush ruffian named Bill. Bill failed to turn up, and the only moisture was that which was induced by the heat. I have left out the 'sad Australian sunset' because the sun was not going down at the time. The burial took place exactly at mid-day.

The dead bushman's name was Jim, apparently; but they found no portraits, nor locks of hair, nor any love letters, nor anything of that kind in his swag – not even a reference to his mother; only some papers relating to union matters. Most of us

1. *bowelless* ['baʊəllɪs] : insensitive, unemotional.
2. *wattle* : Australian acacia tree, often part of the kind of 'romantic' scene satirised here.
3. *grizzled* : with grey hair.
4. *rugged* ['rʌgɪd] : strong and rough.
5. *suspicious moisture* : the wetness in Bill's eyes makes the observer believe that he is close to tears.

didn't know the name till we saw it on the coffin; we knew him as 'that poor chap that got drowned yesterday'.

'So his name's James Tyson,' said my drover acquaintance, looking at the plate.

'Why! Didn't you know that before?' I asked.

'No; but I knew he was a union man.'

It turned out, afterwards, that JT wasn't his real name – only 'the name he went by'.[1]

Anyhow he was buried by it, and most of the 'Great Australian Dailies' have mentioned in their brevity columns[2] that a young man named James John Tyson was drowned in a billabong of the Darling last Sunday.

We did hear, later on, what his real name was; but if we ever chance to read it in the 'Missing Friends Column', we shall not be able to give any information to heart-broken Mother or Sister or Wife, nor to any one who could let him hear something to his advantage – for we have already forgotten the name.

---

1. *the name he went by* : the name by which he chose to be known.
2. *brevity columns* : parts of a newspaper giving very brief news reports.

Characters

1. What do we learn about the dead man? What does Henry Lawson want us to understand by this?

2. There are three individuals who are identified in the course of the story. Write a short description of each.

   i. The drunk shearer;

   ii. The drover;

   iii. The bull-necked publican.

Setting

1. The story moves from one setting to another. Identify these two main settings.

2. All the people mentioned are men. How does this affect the emotional climate of the funeral? What would change if one or more women had been introduced?

3. Find at least three points in the story where Lawson puts emphasis on the heat. What is the effect of this?

4. We learn something from the story, indirectly, about certain social customs in Australia. Find at least two examples.

Structure

The story of the funeral is framed by brief references to the periods preceding and following it. At what points, exactly, does the account of the funeral begin and end?

Symbolism

1. What is suggested by 'dancing jigs' and 'skylarking and fighting' in the second paragraph?

2. What metaphor does Lawson use for the dead body? Do you find it effective?

3. Comment on the absent elements mentioned in the paragraph beginning 'I have left out the wattle'. What is Lawson's purpose in this paragraph?

Language

1. The word 'stranger' is used of various people in the first part of the story. What does it suggest?

2. What evidence is there in the story to suggest that the union men are not religious?

3. Irony is often used to suggest a critical attitude to a person or situation. Give examples of irony from the story and identify the person or situation criticised.

EXAMPLE OF IRONY	WHAT IS CRITICISED

Narrator

1. Although this story is told in the first person, the narrator remains largely uninvolved. Why do you think Lawson chose to use a first-person narrator here?

2. Irony is the technique of saying one thing when you mean another; it is often humorous in effect.

    Re-read the paragraph on p. 61 beginning 'Just here man's ignorance and vanity . . .'. Can you identify an example of irony here?

Themes

1. Is this a story about death or about life? Give reasons for your answer.

2. The title draws attention to the union. How important is this in the course of the story?

The Persimmon Tree

MARJORIE BARNARD

Marjorie Barnard 1897-1987

Born and educated in Sydney, New South Wales, she worked as a librarian as well as writing both fiction and non-fiction. Her first nine books were written in collaboration with her friend Flora Eldershaw, under the joint name of M. Barnard Eldershaw; but it was her independent work, beginning with a collection of short stories published in 1943, that showed her special interest in solitary individuals who experience something similar to what James Joyce called 'epiphanies': moments of intense emotional awareness which illuminate them, often painfully. *The Persimmon Tree*, first published in 1943, is an example of this. It is a delicately written, intimate story which draws on the symbolist tradition: the use of private symbols in literary creation to create a mysterious atmosphere.

I SAW THE SPRING COME ONCE and I won't forget it. Only once. I had been ill all the winter and I was recovering. There was no more pain, no more treatments or visits to the doctor. The face that looked back at me from my old silver mirror was the face of a woman who had escaped. I had only to build up my strength. For that I wanted to be alone, an old and natural impulse. I had been out of things for quite a long time and the effort of returning was still too great. My mind was transparent and as tender as new skin. Everything that happened, even the commonest things, seemed to be happening for the first time, and had a delicate hollow ring [1] like music played in an empty auditorium.

I took a flat in a quiet, blind [2] street, lined with English trees. [3] It was one large room, high ceilinged with pale walls, chaste as a cell in a honey comb, [4] and furnished with the passionless, standardized grace of a fashionable interior decorator. It had the afternoon sun which I prefer because I like my mornings shadowy and cool, the relaxed end of the night prolonged as far as possible. When I arrived the trees were bare and still against

1. *hollow ring* : echoing sound.
2. *blind* : a blind street is one which is closed at one end.
3. *English trees* : trees typical of English towns, not native to Australia.
4. *honey comb* : container made by bees in which to store their honey.

the lilac dusk. There was a block of flats opposite, discreet, well tended, with a wide entrance. At night it lifted its oblongs of rose and golden light far up into the sky. One of its windows was immediately opposite mine. I noticed that it was always shut against the air. The street was wide but because it was so quiet the window seemed near. I was glad to see it always shut because I spend a good deal of time at my window and it was the only one that might have overlooked me and flawed [1] my privacy.

I liked the room from the first. It was a shell that fitted without touching me. The afternoon sun threw the shadow of a tree on my light wall and it was in the shadow that I first noticed that the bare twigs were beginning to swell with buds. A water colour, pretty and innocuous, hung on that wall. One day I asked the silent woman who serviced me to take it down. After that the shadow of the tree had the wall to itself and I felt cleared and tranquil as if I had expelled the last fragment of grit [2] from my mind.

I grew familiar with all the people in the street. They came and went with a surprising regularity and they all, somehow, seemed to be cut to a very correct pattern. [3] They were part of the mise en scene, hardly real at all and I never felt the faintest desire to become acquainted with any of them. There was one woman I noticed, about my own age. She lived over the way. She had been beautiful I thought, and was still handsome with a fine tall figure. She always wore dark clothes, tailor made, and there was reserve in her every movement. Coming and going she was always alone, but you felt that that was by her own choice, that everything she did was by her own steady choice. She walked up the steps so firmly, and vanished so resolutely into the discreet muteness of the building opposite, that I felt a

---

1. *flawed* : made imperfect.
2. *grit* : (here fig.) small cause of irritation.
3. *cut to a . . . pattern* : formed in a specific way.

faint, a very faint, envy of anyone who appeared to have her life so perfectly under control.

There was a day much warmer than anything we had had, a still, warm, milky day. I saw as soon as I got up that the window opposite was open a few inches, 'Spring comes even to the careful heart,' I thought. And the next morning not only was the window open but there was a row of persimmons [1] set out carefully and precisely on the sill, to ripen in the sun. Shaped like a young woman's breasts their deep, rich, golden-orange colour seemed just the highlight that the morning's spring tranquillity needed. It was almost a shock to me to see them there. I remembered at home when I was a child there was a grove of persimmon trees down one side of the house. In the autumn they had blazed deep red, taking your breath away. They cast a rosy light into rooms on that side of the house as if a fire were burning outside. Then the leaves fell and left the pointed dark gold fruit clinging to the bare branches. They never lost their strangeness – magical, Hesperidean [2] trees. When I saw the Fire Bird [3] danced my heart moved painfully because I remembered the persimmon trees in the early morning against the dark windbreak [4] of the loquats. [5] Why did I always think of autumn in springtime?

Persimmons belong to autumn and this was spring. I went to the window to look again. Yes, they were there, they were real. I had not imagined them, autumn fruit warming to a ripe transparency in the spring sunshine. They must have come, expensively packed in sawdust, from California or have lain all winter in storage. Fruit out of season.

1. *persimmons* [pə'sɪmənz] : orange-coloured soft fruit which ripens only after the leaves have fallen from the tree.
2. *Hesperidean* [hɛspə'rɪdɪən] : like the trees producing golden apples which, according to myth, grow in the Islands of the Blessed.
3. *the Fire Bird* : a ballet danced to music by Igor Stravinsky.
4. *windbreak* : a line of trees giving protection from the wind.
5. *loquats* ['ləʊkwɒts] : small yellow Oriental fruit.

It was later in the day when the sun had left the sill that I saw the window opened and a hand come out to gather the persimmons. I saw a woman's figure against the curtains. *She* lived there. It was her window opposite mine.

Often now the window was open. That in itself was like the breaking of a bud. A bowl of thick cream pottery, shaped like a boat, appeared on the sill. It was planted, I think, with bulbs. She used to water it with one of those tiny, long-spouted, [1] handpainted cans that you use for refilling vases, and I saw her gingerly loosening the earth with a silver table fork. She didn't look up or across the street. Not once.

Sometimes on my leisurely walks I passed her in the street. I knew her quite well now, the texture of her skin, her hands, the set of her clothes, her movements. The way you know people when you are sure you will never be put to the test of speaking to them. I could have found out her name quite easily. I had only to walk into the vestibule of her block and read it in the list of tenants, or consult the visiting card on her door. I never did.

She was a lonely woman and so was I. That was a barrier, not a link. Lonely women have something to guard. I was not exactly lonely. I had stood my life on a shelf, that was all. I could have had a dozen friends round me all day long. But there wasn't a friend that I loved and trusted above all the others, no lover, secret or declared. She had, I suppose, some nutrient hinterland on which she drew.

The bulbs in her bowl were shooting. [2] I could see the pale new green spears standing out of the dark loam. I was quite interested in them, wondered what they would be. I expected tulips, I don't know why. Her window was open all day long now, very fine thin curtains hung in front of it and these were never parted. Sometimes they moved but it was only in the breeze.

1. *long-spouted* : the spout is the special opening which allows liquid to be poured out of a container, such as a watering can.
2. *shooting* : (here) putting out their first leaves.

The trees in the street showed green now, thick with budded leaves. The shadow pattern on my wall was intricate and rich. It was no longer an austere winter pattern as it had been at first. Even the movement of the branches in the wind seemed different. I used to lie looking at the shadow when I rested in the afternoon. I was always tired then and so more permeable to impressions. I'd think about the buds, how pale and tender they were, but how implacable. The way an unborn child is implacable. If man's world were in ashes the spring would still come. I watched the moving pattern and my heart stirred with it in frail, half-sweet melancholy.

One afternoon I looked out instead of in. It was growing late and the sun would soon be gone, but it was warm. There was gold dust in the air, the sunlight had thickened. The shadows of trees and buildings fell, as they sometimes do on a fortunate day, with dramatic grace. *She* was standing there just behind the curtains in a long dark wrap, [1] as if she had come from her bath and was going to dress, early, for the evening. She stood so long and so still, staring out – at the budding trees, I thought – that tension began to accumulate in my mind. My blood ticked like a clock. Very slowly she raised her arms and the gown fell from her. She stood there naked, behind the veil of the curtains, the scarcely distinguishable but unmistakeable form of a woman whose face was in shadow.

I turned away. The shadow of the burgeoning [2] bough was on the white wall. I thought my heart would break.

1. *wrap* : dressing-gown without buttons.
2. *burgeoning* : growing rapidly.

Characters

1. How old, approximately, are the two women in this story? How do you know?

2. We never learn the name of either woman. Which of the following is the most probable reason for this, in your opinion?

   i. It gives them both an air of mystery.

   ii. It makes them representative of all women, rather than distinct individuals.

   iii. It creates a sense of emotional distance between the reader and the characters.

   Explain the reasons for your choice.

Setting

1. Trees are an important element in the setting of this story: they are part of the environment in which the narrator lives, and part of her memory of childhood. Find and underline the various references to trees. What do they contribute to the story?

2. The narrator responds particularly to shadows. What does this suggest to you about her? How does it relate to the use of colour in the narrative?

Structure

1. The story relates the coming of spring, but it contains a number of references to autumn. Why should this be so?

2. There is one element which is usually found in narrative fiction but which is missing here. What is it? Why do you think the author chose not to use it?

Symbolism

1. Give your interpretation of the symbols listed below:

    i.   the persimmons on the window sill (p. 71);
    ii. the bowl planted with bulbs (p. 72);
    iii. the shadow of the bough on the wall (p. 73).

2. 'If man's world were in ashes the spring would still come' (p. 73). This is literally true, but it also has symbolic significance here. In what sense does it express the meaning of the story as a whole?

3. Suggest a reason for the title. What does the persimmon tree symbolise?

Language

1. Which of the following are similes, and which are metaphors?

    i.   my mind was transparent and tender as new skin.
    ii. chaste as a cell in a honey comb.
    iii. I liked the room from the first. It was a shell that fitted without touching me.
    iv. a still, warm, milky day.
    v.   Often now the window was open. That in itself was like the breaking of a bud.
    vi. I had stood my life on a shelf.
    vii. She had, I suppose, some nutrient hinterland on which she drew.

    Is there one which you find particularly effective? Why?

2. What does the narrator mean when she thinks 'Spring comes even to the careful heart' (p. 71)?

3. Why is the word 'she' italicised on p. 72?

Narrator

1. Which of the following is an accurate description of this story?

   i. It is told by an omniscient narrator.

   ii. It is told in the third person, from the point of view of one character.

   iii. It is told in the first person.

2. Is the narrator a happy person? Give reasons for your answer.

Themes

1. The narrator is represented as recovering from a serious illness. If this element were omitted, would the story be changed in any important way?

2. The last paragraph is charged with an almost unbearable emotion. Why is the narrator so moved at this point? What is the significance of 'the shadow of the burgeoning bough' in emotional terms?

Canada

The Summer
My Grandmother Was
Supposed To Die

MORDECAI RICHLER

Mordecai Richler 1931-

The Richler family originated in Eastern Europe, from where they emigrated to Canada in the early twentieth century to escape anti-Semitism. Born and brought up in Montreal, Mordecai Richler lived for a year in Paris, and then, from 1954 to 1972, in London and subsequently in Israel. On his return to his native city he became an increasingly respected novelist and journalist, who has held a number of visiting professorships in Canadian universities. His journalism and his scripts for films and television have ensured that he has a regular income which allows him to spend time on his novels, for which he has won a number of awards. Richler draws on the linguistic richness of Yiddish, the German-based language used by many Jews in North America and elsewhere, to underline the close-knit, inward-looking nature of the Jewish community in a non-Jewish country and to give liveliness and humour to his dialogue. His novels, like the story included here, cleverly counterpoint satire and pathos.

D R. KATZMAN discovered the gangrene on one of his monthly visits. 'She won't last a month,' he said.

He repeated that the second month, the third, and the fourth, and now she lay dying in the heat of the back bedroom.

'If only she'd die,' my mother said. 'Oh God, why doesn't she die? God in heaven, what's she holding on for?'

The summer my grandmother was supposed to die we did not chip in [1] with the Breenbaums to take a cottage in the Laurentians. [2] It wouldn't have been practical. The old lady couldn't be moved, the nurse came daily and the doctor twice a week, and so it seemed best to stay in the city and wait for her to die or, as my mother said, pass away. It was a hot summer, her bedroom was just behind the kitchen, and when we sat down to eat we could smell her. The dressings on my grandmother's left leg had to be changed several times a day and, according to Dr. Katzman, her condition was hopeless. 'It's in the hands of the Almighty,' he said.

'It won't be long now,' my father said, 'and she'll be better off, if you know what I mean.'

'Please,' my mother said.

1. *chip in* : pay a share of the expenses.
2. *the Laurentians* : hills not far from Montreal.

A nurse came every day from the Royal Victorian Order. [1] She arrived punctually at noon and at five to twelve I'd join the rest of the boys under the outside staircase to look up her dress as she climbed to our second-storey flat. Miss Monohan favoured lacy pink panties and that was better than waiting under the stairs for Cousin Bessie, for instance. She wore enormous cotton bloomers, [2] rain or shine. [3]

I was sent out to play as often as possible, because my mother felt it was not good for me to see somebody dying. Usually I'd just roam the scorched streets shooting the breeze. [4] There was Arty, Gas sometimes, Hershey, Stan, and me. We talked about everything from A to Z.

'Why is it,' Arty wanted to know, 'that Tarzan never shits?'

'Dick Tracy too.'

'Or Wonder Woman.'

'She's a dame.' [5]

'So?'

'Jees, wouldn't it be something if Superman crapped [6] in the sky? He could just be flying over Waverly Street when, whamo, [7] Mr. Rabinovitch catches it right in the kisser.' [8]

Mr. Rabinovitch was our Hebrew teacher.

'But there's Tarzan,' Arty insisted, 'in the jungle, week in and week out, and never once does he need to go to the toilet. It's not real, that's all.'

1. *Royal Victorian Order* : a nursing association whose members attend patients in their homes.

2. *bloomers* : long loose trousers worn under a skirt.

3. *rain or shine* : at all times, in all conditions.

4. *shooting the breeze* : (slang) talking informally.

5. *dame* : (North American slang) woman.

6. *crapped* : (vulgar slang) evacuated the bowels.

7. *whamo* [wæməʊ] : (slang) exclamation to suggest the sound made by a sudden blow.

8. *kisser* : (slang) face.

Arty told me, 'Before your grandma dies she's going to roll her eyes and gurgle. That's what they call the death-rattle.'

'Aw, you know everything. Big shot.'[1]

'I *read* it, you jerk,'[2] Arty said, whacking me one,[3] 'in Perry Mason.'

Home again I'd find my mother weeping.

'She's dying by inches,' she said to my father one stifling night 'and none of them even come to see her. Oh, such children! They should only rot in hell.'

'They're not behaving right. It's certainly not according to Hoyle,'[4] my father said.

'When I think of all the money and effort that went into making a rabbi out of Israel[5] – the way Mother doted on him – and for what? Oh, what's the world coming to? God.'

'It's not right.'

Dr. Katzman was amazed. 'I never believed she'd last this long. Really, it must be will-power alone that keeps her going. And your excellent care.'

'I want her to die, Doctor. That's not my mother in the back room. It's an animal. I want her to please please die.'

'Hush. You don't mean it. You're tired.' And Dr. Katzman gave my father some pills for my mother to take. 'A remarkable woman,' he said. A born nurse.'

At night in bed my brother Harvey and I used to talk about our grandmother. 'After she dies,' I said, 'her hair will go on growing for another twenty-four hours.'

---

1. *big shot* : (informal) important person (here used ironically).

2. *jerk* : (slang) stupid, inferior person.

3. *whacking me one* : (informal) hitting me once.

4. *not according to Hoyle* : not according to the rules, not correct (from Edmund Hoyle, the man who set down the rules of poker and many other card games).

5. *Israel* : the name of a brother.

'Sez who?' [1]

'Arty. It's a scientific fact. Do you think Uncle Lou will come from New York for the funeral?'

'Sure.'

'Boy, that means another fiver [2] for me. You too.'

'You shouldn't say things like that, kiddo, [3] or *her ghost will come back to haunt you*.'

'Well,' I said, 'I'll be able to go to her funeral, anyway. I'm not too young any more.'

I was only six years old when my grandfather died, and I wasn't allowed to go to his funeral.

I have only one memory of my grandfather. Once he called me into his study, set me down on his lap, and made a drawing of a horse for me. On the horse he drew a rider. While I watched and giggled he gave the rider a beard and the round fur-trimmed cap of a rabbi.

My grandfather was a Zaddik, [4] one of the Righteous, and I've been told that to study Talmud [5] with him had been a rare pleasure. I wasn't allowed to go to his funeral, but years later I was shown the telegrams of condolence that had come from Eire and Poland and Israel and even Japan. My grandfather had written many books: a translation of the Zohar [6] into modern Hebrew – some twenty years' work – and lots of slender

1. *sez who?* : (slang = says who? who says that?) used to indicate disbelief. Muttel takes it literally in this case.

2. *fiver* : a banknote worth five Canadian dollars.

3. *kiddo* : (informal) form of address for a boy or young man.

4. *Zaddik* : (Hebrew) term of respect for particularly wise and saintly elders.

5. *Talmud* : (Hebrew) compendium of analysis and commentary on the Torah, the Jewish Law, collected over more than a thousand years.

6. *Zohar* : (Hebrew) commentary on the Torah with 'hidden meanings' found especially through numerology.

volumes of sermons, chassidic tales,[1] and rabbinical commentaries. His books had been published in Warsaw and later in New York. He had been famous.

'At the funeral,' my mother told me, 'they had to have six motorcycle policemen to control the crowds. It was such a heat that twelve women fainted – and I'm *not* counting Mrs. Waxman from upstairs. With her, you know, *anything* to fall into a man's arms. Even Pinsky's. And did I tell you that there was even a French-Canadian priest there?'

'No kidding?'

'The priest was a real big *knacker*.[2] A bishop maybe. He used to study with the *zeyda*. The *zeyda* was some personality, you know. Spiritual and wordly-wise at the same time. Such personalities they don't make any more. Today, rabbis and peanuts are the same size.'

But, according to my father, the *zeyda* (his father-in-law) hadn't been as famous as all that. 'There are things I could say,' he told me. 'There was another side to him.'

My grandfather had come from generations and generations of rabbis, his youngest son was a rabbi, but none of his grandchildren would be one. My brother Harvey was going to be a dentist and at the time, 1937, I was interested in flying and my cousin Jerry was already a communist. I once heard Jerry say, 'Our grandpappy wasn't all he was cracked up to be.'[3] When the men at the kosher[4] bakeries went on strike he spoke up against them on the streets where they were picketing and in the *shule*.[5] It was of no consequence to him that they were

1. *chassidic tales* : stories in the form of parables and anecdotes encapsulating a sort of folk version of the Jewish religion.
2. *knacker* [knɑːkəɹ] : (Yiddish) important person.
3. *cracked up to be* : generally believed to be.
4. *kosher* : (Hebrew) approved by the laws of Judaism.
5. *shule* : (Yiddish) synagogue.

grossly underpaid. His superstitious followers had to have bread. 'Grandpappy,' Jerry said, 'was a prize reactionary.'[1]

A week after my grandfather died my grandmother suffered a stroke. Her right side was completely paralysed. She couldn't speak. At first, it's true, my grandmother could say a few words and move her right hand enough to write her name in Hebrew. Her name was Malka. But her condition soon began to deteriorate.

My grandmother had six children and seven step-children, for my grandfather had been married before. His first wife had died in the old country. Two years later he had married my grandmother, the only daughter of the richest man in the village, and their marriage had been a singularly happy one. My grandmother had been a beautiful girl. She had also been a wise, resourceful, and patient wife. Qualities, I fear, indispensable to life with a Zaddik. For the synagogue had paid my grandfather no stipulated salary and much of the money he had picked up here and there he had habitually distributed among rabbinical students, needy immigrants, and widows. A vice, and such it was to his hard-pressed family, which made him as unreliable a provider as a drunkard. And indeed, to carry the analogy further, my grandmother had had to make many hurried trips to the pawnbroker with her jewellery. Not all of it had been redeemed, either. But her children had been looked after. The youngest, her favourite, was a rabbi in Boston, the eldest was the actor-manager of a Yiddish theatre in New York, and another was a lawyer. One daughter lived in Toronto, two in Montreal. My mother was the youngest daughter, and when my grandmother had her stroke there was a family meeting and it was decided that my mother would take care of her. This was my father's fault. All the other husbands spoke up – they protested their wives had too much work, they could never

1. *a prize reactionary* : a perfect example of someone who does not want change.

manage it – but my father detested quarrels, and he was silent. So my grandmother came to stay with us.

Her bedroom, the back bedroom, had actually been promised to me for my seventh birthday. But all that was forgotten now, and I had to go on sharing a bedroom with my brother Harvey. So naturally I was resentful when each morning I left for school my mother said, 'Go in and kiss the *baba* goodbye.'

All the same I'd go into the bedroom and kiss my grandmother hastily. She'd say 'Buoyo-bouyo,' for that was the only sound she could make. And after school it was, 'Go in and tell the *baba* you're home.'

'I'm home, *baba*.'

During those first hopeful months – 'Twenty years ago who would have thought there'd be a cure for diabetes?' my father asked, 'where there's life there's hope, you know' – she'd smile at me and try to speak, her eyes charged with effort. And even later there were times when she pressed my head urgently to her bosom with her surprisingly strong left arm. But as her illness dragged on and on and she became a condition in the house, something beyond hope or reproach, like the leaky icebox, there was less recognition and more ritual in those kisses. I came to dread her room. A clutter of sticky medicine bottles and the cracked toilet chair beside the bed; glazed but imploring eyes and a feeble smile, the wet slap of her lips against my cheeks. I flinched from her touch. After two years of it I protested to my mother. 'Look, what's the use of telling her I'm going or I'm here. She doesn't even recognize me any more.'

'Don't be fresh. [1] She's your grandmother.'

My uncle who was in the theatre in New York sent money regularly to help support my grandmother and, for the first few months, so did the other children. But once the initial and sustaining excitement had passed and it became likely that my

---

1. *fresh* : (North American) disrespectful.

grandmother might linger in her invalid condition for two or maybe even three more years, the cheques began to drop off, and the children seldom came to our house any more. Anxious weekly visits – 'and how is she today, poor lamb?' – quickly dwindled to a dutiful monthly looking in, then a semi-annual visit, and these always on the way to somewhere.

'The way they act,' my father said, 'you'd think that if they stayed long enough to take off their coats we'd make them take the baba home with them.'

When the children did come to visit, my mother made it difficult for them.

'It's killing me,' she said. 'I have to lift her on to that chair three times a day maybe. Have you any idea how heavy she is? And what makes you think I always catch her in time? Sometimes I have to change her bed twice a day. That's a job I'd like to see your wife do,' she said to my uncle, the rabbi.

'We could send her to the Old People's Home,' the rabbi said.

'Now there's an idea,' my father said.

But my mother began to sob. 'Not as long as I'm alive,' she said. And she gave my father a stony [1] look. 'Say something.'

'It wouldn't be according to Hoyle.'

'You want to be able to complain to everyone in town about all the other children,' the rabbi said. 'You've got a martyr complex.'

'Everybody has a point of view, you know. You know what I mean?' my father said. 'So what's the use of fighting?'

Meanwhile, Dr. Katzman came once a month to examine my grandmother. 'It's remarkable, astonishing,' he'd say each time. 'She's as strong as a horse.'

'Some life for a person,' my father said. 'She can't speak – she doesn't recognize anybody – what is there for her?'

The doctor was a cultivated man; he spoke often for women's clubs, sometimes on Yiddish literature and other

---

1. *stony* : showing no friendliness or sympathy.

times, his rubicund face hot with impatience, the voice taking on a doomsday tone, [1] on the cancer threat.

'Who are we to judge?' he asked.

Every evening, during the first months of my grandmother's illness, my mother read her a story by Sholem Aleichem. [2] 'Tonight she smiled,' my mother would say. 'She understood. I can tell.' And my father, my brother, and I, would not comment. Once a week my mother used to give the old lady a manicure. Sunny afternoons she'd lift her into a wheel chair and put her out in the sun. Somebody always had to stay in the house in case my grandmother called. Often, during the night, she would begin to wail unaccountably, and my mother would get up and rock the old lady in her arms for hours. But in the fourth year of my grandmother's illness the strain and fatigue began to tell on my mother. Besides looking after my grandmother – 'and believe you me,' the doctor assured her with a clap on the back, 'it would be a full-time job for a professional nurse' – she had to keep house for a husband and two sons. She began to quarrel with my father and she became sharp with Harvey and me. My father started to spend his evenings playing pinochle [3] at Tansky's Cigar & Soda. Weekends he took Harvey and me to visit his brothers and sisters. And everywhere he went people had little bits of advice for him.

'Sam, you might as well be a bachelor. You're just going to have to put your foot down [4] for once.'

'Yeah, in your face maybe.'

My cousin Libby, who was at McGill, said, 'This could have a very damaging effect on the development of your boys. These are their formative years, Uncle Samuel, and the omnipresence of death in the house . . .'

1. *a doomsday tone* : a tone suggesting disaster. 'Doomsday' is another name for the Day of Judgement.

2. *Sholem Aleichem* : well-known Yiddish writer (1859-1916) of stories full of compassion, irony and humour.

3. *pinochle* : a card game.

4. *put your foot down* : insist on your own idea.

'What you need,' my father said, 'is a boy friend. *And how.*'

At Tansky's Cigar & Soda it was, 'Come clean,[1] Sam. It's no hardship. If I know you, the old lady's got a big insurance policy and when the time comes . . .'

My mother lost lots of weight. After dinner she'd fall asleep in her chair in the middle of Lux Radio Theatre.[2] One minute she'd be sewing a patch on my breeches or be making a list of girls to call for a bingo party (proceeds[3] for the Talmud Torah),[4] and the next she'd be snoring. Then, one morning, she just couldn't get out of bed, and Dr. Katzman came round a week before his regular visit. 'Well, well, this won't do, will it?' He sat in the kitchen with my father and the two men drank apricot brandy out of small glasses.

'Your wife is a remarkable woman,' Dr. Katzman said.

'You don't say?'

'She's got a gallstone[5] condition.'

My father shrugged. 'Have another one for the road,'[6] he said.

'Thank you, but I have several more calls to make.' Dr. Katzman rose, sighing. 'There she lies in that back room, poor old woman,' he said, 'hanging desperately onto life. There's food for thought there.'

 My grandmother's children met again, and the five of them sat around my mother's bed embarrassed, irritated, and quick to take insult. All except my uncle who was in the theatre. He sucked a cigar and drank whisky. He teased my mother, the rabbi, and my aunts, and if not for him I think they would have

---

1. *come clean* : admit the truth.
2. *Lux Radio Theatre* : a series of plays broadcast on the radio and sponsored by the soap manufacturers, Lux.
3. *proceeds* ['prəʊsiːdz] : money obtained through a specific event or activity.
4. *Talmud Torah* : (Hebrew) Hebrew school.
5. *gallstone* : small, painful obstruction in one of the digestive organs, the gall bladder.
6. *one for the road* : a last drink before leaving.

been at each other's throats. It was decided, over my mother's protests, to send my grandmother to the Old People's Home on Esplanade Street. An ambulance came to take my grandmother away and Dr. Katzman said, 'It's for the best.' But my father had been in the back bedroom when the old lady had held on tenaciously to the bedpost, not wanting to be moved by the two men in white – 'Easy does it, granny,' the younger one had said – and afterwards he could not go in to see my mother. He went out for a walk.

'She looked at me with such a funny expression,' he told my brother. 'Is it my fault?'

My mother stayed in bed for another two weeks. My father cooked for us and we hired a woman to do the housework. My mother put on weight quickly, her cheeks regained their normal pinkish hue and, for the first time in months, she actually joked with Harvey and me. She became increasingly curious about our schools and whether or not we shined our shoes regularly. She began to cook again, special dishes for my father, and she resumed old friendships with women on the parochial school board. The change reflected on my father. Not only did his temper improve, but he stopped going to Tansky's every other night, and began to come home early from work. Life at home had never been so rich. But my grandmother's name was never mentioned. The back bedroom remained empty and I continued to share a room with Harvey. I couldn't see the point and so one evening I said, 'Look, why don't I move into the back bedroom?'

My father glared at me across the table.

'But it's empty like.'

My mother left the table. And the next afternoon she put on her best dress and coat and new spring hat.

'Where are you going?' my father asked.

'To see my mother.'

'Don't go looking for trouble.'

'It's been a month. Maybe they're not treating her right.'

'They're experts.'

'Did you think I was never going to visit her? I'm not inhuman, you know.'

'All right, go,' he said.

But after she'd gone my father went to the window and said, 'Son-of-a-bitch.' [1]

Harvey and I sat outside on the steps watching the cars go by. My father sat on the balcony above, cracking peanuts. It was six o'clock, maybe later, when the ambulance turned the corner, slowed down, and parked right in front of the house.

'Son-of-a-bitch,' my father said. 'I knew it.'

My mother got out first, her eyes red and swollen, and hurried upstairs to make my grandmother's bed.

'I'm sorry, Sam, I had to do it.'

'You'll get sick again, that's what.'

'You think she doesn't recognize people. From the moment she saw me she cried and cried. Oh, it was terrible.'

'They're experts there. They know how to handle her better than you do.'

'Experts? Expert murderers you mean. She's got bedsores, [2] Sam. Those dirty little Irish nurses they don't change her linen often enough, they hate her. She must have lost twenty pounds there.'

'Another month and you'll be flat on your back again.'

'Sam, what could I do? Please Sam.'

'She'll outlive all of us. Even Muttel. I'm going out for a walk.'

She was back and I was to blame.

My father became a regular at Tansky's Cigar & Soda again and every morning I had to go in and kiss my grandmother. She began to look like a man. Little hairs had sprouted on her chin, she had a spiky grey moustache and, of course, she was practically bald. This near-baldness, I guess, sprang from the fact that she had been shaving her head ever since she had

---

1. *son-of-a-bitch* : (here) exclamation of dismay.
2. *bedsores* : painful areas on the skin, caused by lying in bed for a long time.

married my grandfather the rabbi. My grandmother had four different wigs, but she had not worn one since the first year of her illness. She wore a little pink cap instead. And so, as before, she said, 'buoyo-buoyo,' to everything.

Once more uncles and aunts sent five-dollar bills, though erratically, to help pay for my grandmother's support. Elderly people, former followers of my grandfather, came to inquire after the old lady's health. They sat in the backroom with her for hours, leaning on their canes, talking to themselves, rocking, always rocking to and fro. 'The Holy Shakers,' my father called them, and Harvey and I avoided them, because they always wanted to pinch our cheeks, give us a dash of snuff [1] and laugh when we sneezed, or offer us a sticky old candy from a little brown bag with innumerable creases in it. When the visit was done the old people would unfailingly sit in the kitchen with my mother for another hour, watching her make lockshen [2] or bake bread. My mother always served them lemon tea and they would talk about my grandfather, recalling his books, his sayings, and his charitable deeds.

And so another two years passed, with no significant change in my grandmother's condition. But fatigue, bad temper, and even morbidity enveloped my mother again. She fought with her brothers and sisters and once, when I stepped into the living-room, I found her sitting with her head in her hands, and she looked up at me with such anguish that I was frightened.

'What did I do now?' I asked.

'If, God forbid, [3] I had a stroke, would you send me to the Old People's Home?'

'Don't be a joke. Of course not.'

'I hope that never in my life do I have to count on my children for anything.'

---

1. *a dash of snuff* : a small quantity of powdered tobacco.
2. *lockshen* : (Yiddish) flat strips of pasta used for soup.
3. *God forbid* : let us hope it won't happen.

The summer my grandmother was supposed to die, the seventh year of her illness, my brother took a job as a shipper [1] and he kept me awake at night with stories about the factory. 'What we do, see, is clear out the middle of a huge pile of lengths of material. That makes for a kind of secret cave. A hideout. Well, then you coax one of the *shiksas* [2] inside and hi-diddle-diddle.' [3]

One night Harvey waited until I had fallen asleep and then he wrapped himself in a white sheet, crept up to my bed, and shouted, 'Bouyo-bouyo.'

I hit him. He shouted.

'Children. Children, please,' my mother called. 'I must get some rest.'

As my grandmother's condition worsened – from day to day we didn't know when she'd die – I was often sent out to eat at my aunt's or at my other grandmother's house. I was hardly ever at home. On Saturday mornings I'd get together with the other guys and we'd walk all the way past the mountain to Eaton's, which was our favourite department store for riding up and down escalators and stealing.

In those days they let boys into the left-field bleachers [4] free during the week and we spent many an afternoon at the ball park. The Montreal Royals, part of the Dodger farm system, [5] was some ball club too. There was Jackie Robinson and Roy Campanella, Honest John Gabbard, Chuck Connors, and Kermit Kitman was our hero. It used to kill us to see that crafty little

1. *shipper* : someone working in a company which exports goods by ship.
2. *shiksas* : (Hebrew) non-Jewish girls.
3. *hi-diddle-diddle* : exclamation used here to mean 'you can do whatever you like'.
4. *left-field bleachers* : cheap unroofed seats on the left side of the baseball field.
5. *farm system* : the Montreal Royals were one of the secondary teams in the group led by the Dodgers.

hebe [1] running around there with all those tall dumb goyim. [2] 'Hey, Kitman,' we'd yell. 'Hey, hey, sho-head, [3] if your father knew you played ball on *shabus* – ' [4] Kitman, unfortunately, was all field and no hit. [5] He never made the majors. 'There goes Kermit Kitman,' we'd yell, after he'd gone down swinging again, 'the first Jewish strike-out king [6] of the International League.' This we usually followed up by bellowing some choice imprecations in Yiddish.

It was after one of these games on a Friday afternoon, that I came home to find a small crowd gathered in front of the house.

'That's the grandson.'

'Poor kid.'

Old people stood silent and expressionless across the street staring at our front door. A taxi pulled up and my aunt hurried out, hiding her face in her hands.

'After so many years,' somebody said.

'And probably next year they'll discover a cure. Isn't that *always* the case?'

I took the stairs two at a time. The flat was full. Uncles and aunts from my father's side of the family, odd old people, Dr. Katzman, Harvey, neighbours, were all standing around and talking in hushed voices in the living-room. I found my father in the kitchen, getting out the apricot brandy. 'Your grandmother's dead,' he said.

'She didn't suffer,' somebody said. 'She passed away in her sleep.'

'A merciful death.'

1. *hebe* : abbreviation for Hebrew, a Jew.
2. *goyim* : (Hebrew) Gentiles, non-Jews.
3. *sho-head* : (slang) idiot.
4. *shabus* : (Hebrew) the Sabbath (Saturday, the Jewish holy day, on which Orthodox Jews do not travel or play games).
5. *all field and no hit* : a player who did not score many points.
6. *strike-out king* : baseball player most often put out as a result of three unsuccessful hits.

'Where's Maw?'

'In the bedroom with . . . you'd better not go in,' my father said.

'I want to see her.'

My mother's face was long with grief. She wore a black shawl, and glared down at a knot of handkerchief clutched in a fist that had been cracked by washing-soda. 'Don't come in here,' she said.

Several bearded, round-shouldered men in black shiny coats stood round the bed. I couldn't see my grandmother.

'Your grandmother's dead.'

'Daddy told me.'

'Go and wash your face and comb your hair. You'll have to get your own supper.'

'O.K.'

'One minute. The *baba* left some jewellery. The ring is for Harvey's wife and the necklace is for yours.'

'Who's getting married?'[1]

'Better go and wash your face. And remember behind the ears, Muttel.'

Telegrams were sent, long-distance calls were made, and all through the evening relatives and neighbours came and went like swarms of fish when crumbs have been dropped into the water.

'When my father died,' my mother said, 'they had to have six motorcycle policemen to control the crowds. Twelve people fainted, such a heat . . .'

The man from the funeral parlour came.

'There goes the only Jewish businessman in town,' my Uncle Harry said, 'who wishes all his customers were Germans.'

'This is no time for jokes.'

'Listen, life goes on.'

My Cousin Jerry had begun to use a cigarette holder.

---

1.   *Who's getting married?* : rhetorical question meaning 'I have no plans to get married'. The use of ironic questions of this kind is typical of North American Jewish speech.

'Everyone's going to be sickeningly sentimental,' he said. 'Soon the religious mumbo-jumbo[1] starts. I can hardly wait.'

Tomorrow was the Sabbath and so, according to the law, my grandmother couldn't be buried until Sunday. She would have to lie on the floor all night. Two old grizzly[2] women in white came to move and wash the body and a professional mourner arrived to sit up and pray for her.

'I don't trust his face,' my mother said. 'He'll fall asleep. You watch him, Sam.'

'A fat lot of good prayers will do her now.'

'Will you just watch him, please.'

'I'll watch him, I'll watch him.' My father was livid[3] about my Uncle Harry. 'The way he's gone after that apricot brandy you'd think that guy never saw a bottle in his life before.'

Harvey and I were sent to bed, but we couldn't sleep. My aunt was sobbing over the body in the living-room – 'That dirty hypocrite,' my mother said – there was the old man praying, coughing, and spitting into his handkerchief each time he woke; and hushed voices and whimpering from the kitchen, where my father and mother sat. Harvey was in a good mood, he let me have a few puffs of his cigarette.

'Well, kiddo, this is our last night together. Tomorrow you can take over the back bedroom.'

'*Are you crazy?*'

'You always wanted it for yourself.'

'She died in there, but. You think I'm going to sleep in there?'

'Good night. Happy dreams, kiddo.'

'Hey, let's talk some more.'

Harvey told me a ghost story. 'Did you know that when they hang a man,' he said, 'the last thing that happens is that he has an orgasm?'

---

1. *mumbo-jumbo* : (informal) mysterious, apparently meaningless words or activity.
2. *grizzly* : very unpleasant. The more usual spelling is 'grisly'.
3. *livid* : very angry.

'A what?'

'Forget it. I forgot you were still in kindergarten.'[1]

'I know plenty. Don't worry.'

'At the funeral they're going to open her coffin to throw dirt in her face. It's supposed to be earth from Eretz.[2] They open it and you're going to have to look.' Harvey stood up on his bed, holding his hands over his head like claws. He made a hideous face. 'Bouyo-buoyo. Who's that sleeping in my bed? Woo-Woo.'

My uncle who was in the theatre, the rabbi, and my aunt from Toronto, all came to Montreal for the funeral. Dr. Katzman came too.

'As long as she was alive,' my mother said, 'he couldn't even send five dollars a month. Some son! What a rabbi! I don't want him in my house, Sam. I can't bear the sight of him.'

'You don't mean a word of that and you know it,' Dr. Katzman said.

'Maybe you'd better give her a sedative,' the rabbi said.

'Sam. Sam, will you say something, please.'

My father stepped up to the rabbi, his face flushed. 'I'll tell you this straight to your face, Israel,' he said. 'You've gone down in my estimation.'

'Really,' the rabbi said, smiling a little.

My father's face burned a deeper red. 'Year by year,' he said, 'your stock has gone down with me.'[3]

And my mother began to weep bitterly, helplessly, without control. She was led unwillingly to bed. While my father tried his best to comfort her, as he said consoling things, Dr. Katzman plunged a needle into her arm. 'There we are,' he said.

1. *kindergarten* : the first year of formal education, usually at the age of five. Harvey is suggesting that Muttel is very childish and inexperienced.

2. *Eretz* : (Hebrew) abbreviated form of Eretz Yisroel, the land of Israel, the homeland of the Jews.

3. *your stock has gone down with me* : I have had less and less respect for you.

I went to sit in the sun on the outside stairs with Arty. 'I'm going to the funeral,' I said.

'I couldn't go anyway.'

Arty was descended from the tribe of high priests and so was not allowed to be in the presence of a dead body. I was descended from the Yisroelis. [1]

'The lowest of the low,' Arty said.

'Aw.'

My uncle, the rabbi, and Dr. Katzman stepped into the sun to light cigarettes.

'It's remarkable that she held out [2] for so long,' Dr. Katzman said.

'Remarkable?' my uncle said. 'It's written that if a man has been married twice he will spend as much time with his first wife in heaven as he did on earth. My father, may he rest in peace, was married to his first wife for seven years and my mother, may she rest in peace, has managed to keep alive for seven years. Today in heaven she will be able to join my father, may he rest in peace.'

Dr. Katzman shook his head, he pursed his lips. 'It's amazing,' he said. 'The mysteries of the human heart. Astonishing.'

My father hurried outside. 'Dr. Katzman, please. It's my wife. Maybe the injection wasn't strong enough? She just doesn't stop crying. It's like a tap. Could you come please?'

'Excuse me,' Dr. Katzman said to my uncle.

'Of course.'

My uncle approached Arty and me.

'Well, boys,' he said, 'what would you like to be when you grow up?'

---

1. *Yisroelis* : one of the less aristocratic Hebrew tribes.
2. *held out* : survived, resisted.

Characters

1. What are the narrator's mother's most positive attributes? What are her weaknesses? Quote from the text to justify your answers.

2. Who is the dominant partner in the marriage of the narrator's parents? Explain your choice.

3. In what respects are the narrator's reactions typical of a child? Give at least three examples.

4. Does the grandmother have a discernible personality?

Setting

1. Comment on the significance of the grandmother's bedroom

   i. for the narrator;

   ii. for his mother.

2. What have you learned from this story about the community in which the narrator lives? Make notes especially on:

   i. attitude to family;

   ii. relationships between children and adults;

   iii. concept of duty.

Structure

1. There is no conventional introduction to this story. Do you find the opening paragraph effective? Give your reasons.

2. The story is divided into five sections. Summarise each section in the chart on the next page. The first one has been started to help you.

Section 1	pp. 81-4	The doctor predicts the old lady's death and her family . . .
Section 2		
Section 3		
Section 4		
Section 5		

3. In many passages of dialogue, we are not directly told who is speaking. Identify the speakers in the passage from 'My father glared at me across the table' to 'She was back and I was to blame' (pp. 91-9).

Symbolism

1. 'She became increasingly curious about our schools and whether or not we shined our shoes regularly' (p. 91). What is symbolised by this curiosity?

2. Why does the man from the funeral parlour wish all his customers were German? What does this joke refer to?

Language

1. Compare the language used by the children with the language used by the adults. Are all the differences of the same kind?

2. What does the narrator's father mean by 'I knew it' (p. 92)?

3. Dr Katzman uses a particular word over and over again. What is it? What does it suggest about him?

4. Judging from the context, what do the following expressions mean?

   i. zeyda
   ii. baba

5. Read the paragraph beginning 'During those first hopeful months' (p. 87). What words or phrases suggest the narrator's revulsion at visiting his grandmother's room?

Narrator

1. How old, approximately, is Muttel at the time of his grandmother's illness and death? List the elements in the story on which you base your answer.

2. There is frequent use of humour in the narration. Give at least three examples of this and explain how the narrator's age contributes to the humorous effect. Do you find humour distasteful in a story about illness and death?

Themes

1. Write a short essay on the pros and cons of sending old people into residential care when they require constant nursing.

2. Does Muttel love his grandmother? Do you find his attitude to her natural, deplorable, defensible or, perhaps, all three?

3. 'Comedy' is a term used to define literature which sets out to entertain the reader, and usually ends happily. Is this story a comedy?

India

When Sikh
Meets Sikh

Khushwant Singh

Khushwant Singh 1915-

The son of a wealthy family, Singh was born in a part of India which is now Pakistan and had a first-class education in the Indian capital, Delhi, and later at King's College, London, where he qualified as a lawyer. He has also lectured on religion at a number of universities, worked as a journalist for such prestigious newspapers as the *New York Times*, the *Guardian* and the *Times Literary Supplement*, edited several Indian newspapers and been a member of the Indian Parliament. It was while he was working for the Indian High Commission in Canada in the 1940s that he began to write short stories; Canada, he says, is his favourite country, and the story chosen for this volume interestingly combines a Canadian setting with Singh's characteristically humorous portrayal of his own countrymen. He has no time for psychological subtlety, but his eye for the absurd is particularly acute. He is the author of a number of works on Indian history as well as four collections of short stories and three novels.

WHEN A SIKH [1] MEETS ANOTHER SIKH they both say 'Sut Sree Akal,' which means simply 'God is truth.' More frequently one starts loudly proclaiming 'Wah guru jee ka Khalsa,' which means 'The Sikhs are the chosen of God,' and the other joins him in completing it even more loudly with 'Wah guru jee kee Fateh' – 'And victory be to our God.' The latter form of greeting is fast gaining in popularity at the expense of the former. The reason for this is obvious. Just saying God is truth is as pointless as the European habit of referring to the time of the day and prefixing it as good. The other form goes further. It expresses both a truth and a hope. That the Sikhs are the chosen of God is something no Sikh has any doubt about – the Guru himself called them the Khalsa or the elect. And what could be more fitting than wishing victory to one's god all the time?

Although the Sikhs themselves rightly believe that they are the elect, there are other races who consider themselves chosen, other nations which call themselves A-1, [2] and sects which style themselves the salt of the earth. As a matter of fact, in India itself other communities belittle the Sikhs as an odd people and have lots of stories making fun of them. Sikhs ignore these jests and have a lordly sort of superiority which they express in their day-

---

1. *Sikh* [siːk] : a member of a specific Indian religion. All Sikh men wear beards and turbans.
2. *A-1* : first class.

to-day vocabulary. Thus all clean-shaven people are *Kirars*, which literally means cowards, or *Sirghassas*, which means bald-because-of-beating-on-the-head. A Sikh refers to himself as equal to a hundred and twenty-five thousand, or simply as an army.

Sikhs are not just a crude fighting type. Despite the many Victoria and Military Crosses [1] they have won on the field of battle, they are essentially a peace-loving people. They were virtually the first community to prove the efficacy of passive resistance as a political weapon (and, paradoxically, also the first to organise a planned insurrection against British rule). The one thing which really marks them out [2] is their spirit of pioneering. Although they number little over four million, there is hardly a country in the world without a Sikh – except perhaps Saudi Arabia and, now, Pakistan. There are Sikh sentries, policemen and taxi-drivers in all countries from Northern China to Turkey. There are Sikh farmers and artisans in Australia, South Africa, United States, Canada, and the countries of South America. There are Sikh doctors, pedlars [3] and fortune-tellers in every country of Europe.

There is nothing racial or hereditary about the professions the Sikhs choose. A farmer in the Punjab may become a money-lender in Bombay, a carpenter in East Africa, a picker of fruit in California, or a lumberjack in Canada. If necessary, he can train a troupe of love-birds [4] to pick out cards telling fortunes to matelots [5] in Marseilles – or just look more oriental himself and read ladies' hands at fun fairs. If all that fails, he can exploit his

1. *Victoria and Military Crosses* : medals given for exceptional courage in battle.
2. *marks them out* : makes them noticeably different.
3. *pedlars* : people selling small objects door-to-door.
4. *love-birds* : very small kind of parrots.
5. *matelots* ['mætləʊz] : (French) sailors.

fine physique and cash in on [1] feats of endurance. This brings me to the story of my meeting with Narinjan Singh – a farmer in Punjab, a domestic servant in Shanghai, a fruit picker in San Francisco, an accountant in Vancouver, and an all-in wrestler [2] in Toronto. I met him in Toronto.

For several days I had read his name in the papers and on hoardings. [3] He was apparently quite a figure [4] in the Canadian wrestling world and was due to fight someone called Mazurki, a Pole who also acted in the films. Narinjan Singh was known as Nanjo the Villain, Mazurki as Iron Mike. It seemed to be an important fight. In any case, Nanjo promised to be an interesting character. So I went to the auditorium.

The Maple Leaf Garden Auditorium was packed with nearly twenty thousand Canadian men, women and children. When I turned up to buy my ticket a couple of burly Mounted Policemen [5] came up to me and said in a friendly way: 'You be careful.' They escorted me to my seat and one of them stood by in the gangway.

After the preliminary bouts [6] the microphone blared forth: 'Attention please, attention please. We now come to the last fight, between Nanjo Singh of India and Iron Mike Mazurki of Hollywood, California. Time – twenty minutes. Umpire – Steve Borman.'

A tremendous applause went up as the tall, lanky Pole walked down the gangway. He bowed to his admirers and

---

1. *cash in on* : take full financial advantage of.

2. *all-in-wrestler* : participant in a fighting sport in which all kinds of holds are permitted.

3. *hoardings* : high fences on which advertisements are stuck.

4. *he was . . . quite a figure* : he was well-known, a person of some importance.

5. *Mounted Policemen* : policemen in Canada who wear red jackets and work on horseback. They are popularly known as Mounties, see page 111.

6. *bouts* : (here) wrestling matches.

entered the ring, followed by scores [1] of autograph hunters. A minute later came the Indian, in a yellow turban and green dressing gown. The crowd hissed and booed. Unconcerned with the reception, he clambered into his corner, took off his turban and knelt in prayer – Moslem fashion towards Mecca. Then he unrobed. He was a short, squat man with brown bulging muscles, and a broad hairy chest. The umpire spoke to them in the centre of the ring. Then the fight started.

Nanjo was certainly the 'top cad' [2] in the Canadian wrestling world. He was also an excellent actor. A Sikh, he turned to Mecca as the Canadians thought he should. He rudely pushed away autograph hunters and hit a couple of youngsters who made faces at him. In the ring he dug his fingers in his adversary's eyes, pulled his hair and hit him. In fact, he broke all the rules of wrestling and everyone saw him break them barring [3] the umpire (who was not supposed to notice).

'This is all phoney, you know,' my neighbour informed me. 'Actually, Nanjo is as meek as a lamb. Nice guy once you get to know him.'

They all knew it was phoney; but it did not prevent them getting hysterical, when Nanjo twisted Mazurki's arms they shared the Pole's agony with sympathetic 'No! No!s!' When Mazurki had Nanjo squirming under him they yelled: 'Kill the nigger,' So it went on for full fifteen minutes.

'Five minutes to go,' announced the loudspeaker.

My neighbour braced himself [4] and nudged me. 'Now the phoney ends and the fight begins.'

In a trice [5] the Indian flung the lanky Pole, who had been sitting on his chest for the last five minutes, sprawling on the

1. *scores* : large numbers. A score is, literally, twenty.
2. *top cad* : a cad is a man who behaves dishonourably. Nanjo is successful in presenting himself as a cad in the wrestling ring.
3. *barring* : except.
4. *braced himself* : stiffened.
5. *in a trice* : very quickly.

canvas. With a murderous yell he pounced upon Mazurki, caught the man's head between his thighs and twisted his arms behind his back. This was his famous 'cobra hold.' It squashed the head and strangled the victim at the same time. There was a petrified silence in the arena.

A raucous voice rang out: 'Mar dey Saley ko'. Enthusiastically I joined my solitary countryman with a loud 'Mar dey'. There was a shower of empty cigarette cases, paper balls and silver paper on my head and twenty thousand voices roared: 'Shut up.'

My neighbour was nervous. 'You better look out [1] – people get a little worked up, you know.' The Mounty came close to me and warned me: 'Better keep quiet mister, if you want to go home.'

The crowd rose from their seats and clustered round the ring. A woman ran up and put the lighted end of her cigarette on the Indian's ankle. But Nanjo wouldn't let go his victim. The police rushed in to get the spectators back in their seats and formed to cordon round the wrestlers. For some time Mazurki struggled and groaned, then he gave up. The referee stopped the fight and held aloft Nanjo's hand as the victor. The crowd booed and hissed and made towards him. Half-a-dozen stalwart [2] Mounties surrounded the wrestler and hustled him into his dressing room.

A quarter of an hour later, when the crowd had dispersed and it looked safe enough for a bearded and turbaned Indian to venture forth, I made for Nanjo's dressing room to collect some facts of his life. In the over-heated, stuffy room there were more than a dozen hulking masses of fat and flesh – Toronto's leading heavyweights. They were the best of friends. Nanjo and Mazurki were pounding [3] each other's bellies with friendly

1. *You better look out* : you had better be careful.
2. *stalwart* : strong.
3. *pounding* : beating with their fists.

blows and being obscenely intimate – 'You son-ov-a-gun,' 'You son-ov-a-bitch,'[1] and so on.

Nanjo saw me and a broad smile lit his face. 'Holy mackerel[2] – see who's here – feller[3] from my own country.'

I introduced myself and shook several sweaty hands. Nanjo's vocabulary of English words came to an end with 'Jeezez[4] it's good to see you.' Then he broke into pure rustic Punjabi.[5]

'I could floor[6] the lot of them, but my manager won't let me. I have to lose. I have to act as a bad man and am often disqualified for fouling.[7] What can I do?' Then with a characteristically Indian gesture he slapped his stomach. 'All for the belly. But when I have made enough I will show you what I can do. I'll floor the incestuous sister-sleepers.[8] The whole bloody lot of them. Then I will go back to Hoshiarpur and till the land. I want to show my village to my wife.' He looked round the crowded room and shouted for his wife. A buxom[9] blonde with a broad grin that bared[10] several gold teeth

1. *son-ov-a-gun, son-ov-a-bitch* : expressions used between men, sometimes as insults but sometimes, as here, to show affection. The spelling 'ov' for 'of' is used to suggest the men's pronunciation.

2. *holy mackerel* : an exclamation of surprise.

3. *feller* : = fellow, man. Again, the spelling suggests Nanjo's pronunciation.

4. *Jeezez* : = Jesus, here used as an exclamation. Once more the spelling suggests Nanjo's pronunciation.

5. *Punjabi* [pʌn'dʒɑːbi] : an Indian language.

6. *floor* : knock down.

7. *fouling* : doing something which is against the rules.

8. *incestuous sister-sleepers* : a literal translation of an elaborate Punjabi insult.

9. *buxom* : used of a woman who is healthy and attractive, with big breasts.

10. *bared* : exposed.

emerged from the ring of wrestlers and greeted me with a loud 'How dyedo'[1] and vigorous chewing of gum.

'She's Sikh now. Her name is Mahinder Kaur. I've taught her some Punjabi. Baby tell the gentlemen what I taught you.'

The blonde spat out her chewing gum.

'Wah guru jee ka Khalsa.'

'Wah guru jee kee Fateh.'

1. *How dyedo* : How do you do. The spelling suggests the woman's pronunciation.

Characters

1.   There is contradictory evidence of Nanjo's character in the course of the story. Group the following expressions under the headings 'Positive' and 'Negative' (they are listed in the order in which they appear in the story):

   – an interesting character
   – the 'top cad' in the Canadian wrestling world
   – an excellent actor
   – he rudely pushed away . . . faces at him
   – meek as a lamb
   – with a murderous yell he pounced . . .
   – But Nanjo wouldn't let go his victim
   – I have to act as a bad man.

2.   The crowd at the wrestling match is represented as an emotional unit. Find phrases in the story which illustrate this. What impression do they give of Canadians? Do you think this is a fair representation of the average Canadian's personality?

Setting

1.   Choose one or more of the following adjectives to describe the Maple Leaf Auditorium.

chaotic	cheerful	crowded	elegant
enthusiastic	friendly	intellectual	
noisy	quiet	serious	

2.   Why is the wrestlers' dressing room 'over-heated' and 'stuffy'?

Structure

The story falls into three main parts: an introduction to the Sikhs, an account of a wrestling match, and a meeting between two Sikhs. How are these parts linked?

Language

1. No explanation is given of the words 'Mar dey Saley ko'. What do you think they mean, judging from the context?

2. Nanjo is represented as speaking only a little English. What makes it seem that he has learned his English without formal study?

3. In the description of the wrestling match, there are many verbs expressing physical movement or position. Which of the following refer to attack and which refer to defence?

dug	flung	pounced	pulled
sitting	sprawling	squashed	squirming
strangled	struggled	twisted	

Narrator

1. What do the narrator and Nanjo have in common?

2. Do you think the narrator is a frequent visitor to wrestling matches? Give reasons for your answer.

Themes

1. Both the wrestlers in this story are immigrants. What kinds of problems do immigrants face in their adopted country? Does Nanjo seem to have adapted successfully to life in Canada?

2. 'The Sikhs are the chosen of God.' How seriously are we expected to take this in the context of the story?

The Only American
From Our Village

ARUN JOSHI

Arun Joshi 1939-93

Joshi is one of the most important Indian novelists writing in English. Growing up in the period when India was reshaping itself after the years of British domination, he was always aware of the tension between the Indian tribal world and the world of the colonisers, who imposed both the advantages and the disadvantages of their civilisation on a country with a very different culture. The need to find one's own roots is the theme of Joshi's best-known novel, *The Strange Case of Billy Biswas* (1971), in which the protagonist rejects the upper-class background in which he has grown up and finds the integrity of his origins in the primitive jungle tribes. The theme of *The Only American From Our Village* is recognisably related to Billy Biswas in its attack on the false values of Dr. Khanna; but Joshi is compassionate despite his anger.

DR. KHANNA was easily the most outstanding immigrant physicist at the University of Wisconsin. Personally, he considered himself to be the finest of *all* physicists, immigrant or native. He was also among the dozen or so best-dressed men on the campus.

When he was forty Dr. Khanna, his wife Joanne, and their two sons decided to visit India, the country that Dr. Khanna had left 15 years earlier and where his fame had preceded him.

The four week trip was a success by all accounts. [1] He was received by an official of the Council of Scientific Research. He addressed a conference on Inter-planetary radiation and inaugurated three well-attended seminars. He met the President and the Prime Minister. He was offered many jobs each of which he politely declined.

His wife and children were worshipped by his relatives whom they had never met before and for whom they had brought Gillette razors, pop records and a mass of one-dollar neck-ties. [2] The records and the neck-ties were unusable because the relatives had neither record-players nor suits but the razors were greatly prized, especially by the women who saved them for their teen-aged sons.

1. *by all accounts* : according to everyone.
2. *one-dollar neck-ties* : ties bought at a very low price.

The last of the four weeks Mrs. Khanna and the children went off on a sight-seeing tour. Dr. Khanna delivered his final talk at a college in his former home-town.

The talk went well. He was introduced to the audience in glorious terms and the boys stayed quiet which was not natural for them. He was thanked profusely and, it seemed, endlessly by the lecturer in Physics. Some of the audience stopped by on their way out and bid their humble farewell with folded hands. At the end of them all an old man came shuffling along [1] and insisted on shaking Dr. Khanna's hands.

'I am the ashtamp farosh of the town.'

'I am the *ashtamp farosh* of the town,' the old man said staring up at Dr. Khanna. His eyes were heavy with cataract. The grease on his jacket shone in the yellow light. Dr. Khanna looked on, puzzled. The Principal was embarrassed.

---

1. *shuffling along* : walking by dragging his feet.

'Mr. Radhey Mohan,' he explained, 'sells court paper [1] in front of the District Courts.'

'Yes,' the old man repeated. 'I am the *ashtamp farosh* of the town. I knew your father. I am very happy to see you. I came here only to see you because I am only an *ashtamp farosh* and do not understand such matters. Nor do my sons because they are not even matriculates. [2] I have not been out of this town. I live in the village which was also your father's village and is, therefore, *your* village. Ha! Ha! I can take you there if you like.'

'I had been to our village when I was a boy,' said Dr. Khanna hastily. He was glad he could say that because some trick [3] of the old man, a slant [4] of the lips, a glint in the eye, the accent, which had also been his father's, had made him uncomfortable. 'I have been to our village several times,' he repeated.

'I know. When you came with your father, you always came to my house because your father and I were very close to each other, like brothers, and I was not then the *ashtamp farosh* because I had property [5] and I did not have to be an *ashtamp farosh* and I lived in style. Of course, all this does not interest you. I know that.'

There was a pause. The Principal who had been trying to put an end to this unexpected encounter edged Dr. Khanna towards the door. The *ashtamp farosh* put his hand on Dr. Khanna's shoulder and began again. Darkness gathered on the grounds outside.

'He was a good student, the best. I sat at the same desk, so I know. I carved my name on my side of the desk. Your father did not want to spoil the wood so I carved his name on *his* side. Before he died we went and looked for the desk and, believe me,

1. *court paper* : special paper used in courts of law.
2. *matriculates* [məˈtrɪkjʊleɪts] : students who have qualified to enter University.
3. *trick* : (here) characteristic movement or expression.
4. *slant* : (here) position.
5. *property* : (here) land or a house owned by an individual.

it was still there. So were the names. It was very strange. I had
not expected the names to be there. Your father's name is on the
Honours Board, too. Mine is not there, because I failed in
matriculation. But his name is there. If you like we can go and
have a look. He stood third in the state. [1] May be you don't
know it. Standing third in forty thousand boys was no joke. He
won a scholarship as he always did. He wanted to take up a job
but his mother said he must go to college. So he went to Lahore.
I am told he made a mark [2] there. But I don't know. I saw him
only when he came home for vacation. If he had made a mark he
did not let it get to his head. He was always the same with me. I
wanted to know about the dancing girls of Lahore but he did
not know about such things. But he had brains. [3] Even I could
see that. I met him every summer, several summers running.
Then he took a job somewhere. In Lucknow or Kanpur or
Allahabad – I don't know. You must know better. I saw him
when his mother died. He cried a lot. Then he locked up the old
house and went away. I did not see much of him for twenty
years. Only once or twice when he brought you and your sisters
to see the village. He came back after he retired. He looked old,
older than his years, but he was happy. He was very proud of
you. He told everyone what all you had done. He got angry
with me because I was not interested in what you had done. He
used to say you would be a big government man when you
came back. He would say you were coming back in one year, in
two years, any time. Then you got married and he was quiet for
many months. But he started talking again. He said you were
the only American from our village. I asked him once what was
so great about being the only American from our village. He
said it was an honour.

---

1. *stood third in the state* : was the third most successful candidate in
   the qualifying examinations.

2. *made a mark* : was successful.

3. *had brains* : was intelligent.

'Some of us used to go for walks. He talked all the time. And he talked only of you. We got fed up with his talk, to tell you the truth. We had a foot in the grave, [1] all of us. What did we care for your achievements; what you did and what you did not do. I told him so one day. He was angry with me. I suppose I should not have said that. He stopped coming with us. He did not go for walks for a while, then he started to go by himself. He chose different timings and took a different route. But I would see him now and then. He had a stoop. [2] You are developing a stoop similar to his, if you don't mind my saying so.'

The *ashtamp farosh* paused. He seemed to have lost the thread [3] of his thoughts. Then he started again, 'After his retirement he had a shave every other day. We used to go together, to the same barber. He would have his shave first because he did not like to wait. But he had to wait anyway while I had *my* shave. It came to the same thing. But he did not mind that. Some people are strange.

'Then, all at once, he started to shave every day. He also had two shirts made. Two new shirts and a suit. He said it was too costly to have a shave every day in the bazaar, so he bought his own razor. A razor and a cake of soap. I asked him what on earth had got into him? Why in God's name did he *have* to shave every day. He took me aside and said he was expecting a ticket. What ticket? I asked him. He said he was expecting a ticket from you to visit America. A return ticket. He looked at me when he said that and his eyes twinkled.'

The *ashtamp farosh* fidgeted [4] inside his pockets for several moments and pulled out a bidi. He did not light it.

'To tell you the truth I was impressed. Kundan Lal going to

---

1. *had a foot in the grave* : were close to death.
2. *stoop* : tendency to stand or walk with the shoulders bent forward.
3. *lost the thread* : forgotten the logical sequence.
4. *fidgeted* : moved his hands restlessly.

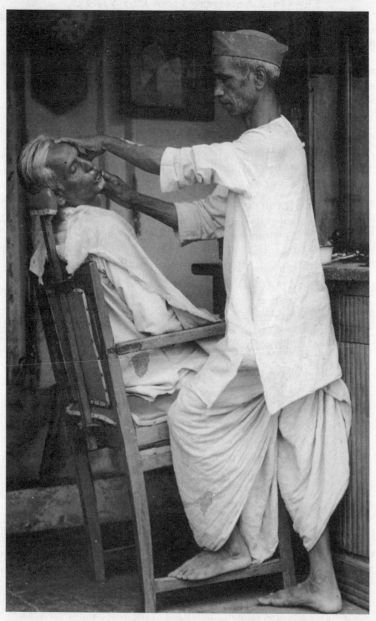

'He would have his shave first because he did not like to wait.'

America, that was not something you could laugh away. [1] I told some fellows about the ticket and before morning the whole village knew about it.

'You see what I mean? Maybe you don't. Maybe you don't have villages like ours in America but you must try to understand what it meant after the whole village knew you were going to send him a ticket. Did you send him a ticket?'

The question took Dr. Khanna by surprise. He looked confused. He said: 'I could not, I did not . . .'

'I thought as much,' said the *ashtamp farosh*, cutting him short. 'Then he did another foolish thing: he turned religious. All his life I had never seen him inside a temple and now he went there every evening. Morning and evening. And that wasn't all. He started even to sing, the old fool. What did he know about singing? Yet he would stand with all those old women and sing, like a donkey, if you don't mind my saying so. I say this only because it hurt me to see him making a fool of himself. I caught hold of him in the street one day and I told him what I thought of him. What do you expect from God, I asked him. Your son? A letter from your son? A ticket? What? Why was he cutting himself off from the rest of us, I asked him. If you were doing well, as he said, what was eating him. [2] Why was he cutting himself off from his friends? I thought he would be angry. But he wasn't. He just stood there in the middle of the street and looked at me, looked right through me as though I were air. Then he went off muttering to himself. I saw him many times after that but I did not speak to him again. I did not want trouble, to tell you the truth. Then he fell ill.'

The *ashtamp farosh* lit his bidi, took a deep pull and, on an impulse, threw it away. Dr. Khanna could see it smouldering in the verandah. The smoke nauseated him. Outside, it was totally

1. *laugh away* : treat as a joke.
2. *what was eating him* : what was troubling him, making him angry.

dark. The winter night had set in. 'Why did you not send him the ticket?' the *ashtamp farosh* asked suddenly. Once again Dr. Khanna was taken by surprise. 'I could not,' he said. 'I did not have the money.'

The *ashtamp farosh* looked at him, puzzled, but he said nothing. 'Nor did your father have the money. So he stayed home and became quiet once again.'

The *ashtamp farosh* fell silent. His expressions became vague. He let his hands drop into his pockets where they fidgeted with a variety of objects.

'Of course he had never had much money. He had a scholarship in school that paid for his fees. But he had only two pyjamas and two kurtas [1] and he had no shoes. We went to school together and came back together. Between the school and our village is the *cho*. Do you remember the *cho*? It runs in the rains. Nine months it is dry. In summer the sand gets very hot. Have you seen how they roast corn in hot sand. You could roast corn in the *cho*. It was half a mile of boiling sand in May that we had to cross. No more, no less. And your father had no shoes. So he would stop this end of the *cho* and take a handful of *dhak* leaves and tie them on his naked feet with a string and he would cross the sand. And if the string came off he would jump around screaming on one foot while I tied the leaves back on to his foot. That is how your father crossed the cho for ten years, Dr. Khanna,' said the *ashtamp farosh*.

His tone was not harsh. [2] He was not even looking at him but somehow Dr. Khanna had the unreasonable feeling that the old man was going to slap him. He wanted to get away and he looked helplessly at the Principal but the *ashtamp farosh* stood between them and the doorway. He had begun to talk again, in a softer voice, as though to himself. 'I told him not to do it. I told him he was being stupid.'

---

1. *kurtas* ['kɔːtəz] : long shirts or tunics worn during the day by Indians.
2. *harsh* : (here) severe, unkind.

After another silence he addressed them again, 'When he fell ill your sister came. He asked me to write to you. I sent you a telegram. It cost me one hundred rupees but you chose to reply only by a letter. I did not understand what you said except that you had to attend some conference. I told your father you had a conference. 'Does he say when he can come?' he asked. I told him you had not said when you could come. 'He must be busy' he said. He did not mention you again. He got better. One day he said, 'Radhey, let us go and look at our old desk.' It was the month of May and it was very hot but he was feeling better and I thought a trip to town will do him good. We went in a rickshaw. [1] And the desk was where it had always been. The same room, the same row, the same place. There were his initials on his side and mine on mine. We went to the Honours Board and had a look at his name. We started back and came to the *cho*. Then the mad thought entered his head. It was madness. No more, no less. There are no words to describe such madness. He even looked mad to me. He stopped the rickshaw before the *cho*. He got off and kicked away his shoes and started plucking at the leaves of *dhak*. He could not tie them because he had arthritis and he could not bend. 'Tie these on my feet, Radhey,' he ordered me. 'You are mad, Kundan Lal,' I told him, but he had a bad look on his face and I knew it was no use arguing with him. I thought he would come to his senses when he touched the boiling sand. But I told you he wasn't himself. [2] He stepped into the *cho*. I followed him carrying his shoes hoping he would stop, shouting at him to stop. I could feel the sand through my soles but told you he had lost his head. He walked the whole half mile. The leaves fell off on the way. God himself could not have stopped him. He had fever by the time he got home. The next day he died.'

1. *rickshaw* ['rɪkʃɔː] : two-wheeled vehicle pulled by one or more persons.
2. *he wasn't himself* : he wasn't in a normal state of mind.

Dr. Khanna winced but his training in the new civilization had been perfect.

'I was very sorry to hear of his death,' he said calmly.

'We must go now, Radhey Mohanji,' said the Principal. He stretched his hand but the *ashtamp farosh* was gone, shuffling through the dark, a bidi in his mouth.

That week-end Dr. Khanna and family boarded a plane for Chicago. At Chicago they changed. As the plane for Madison got aloft Mrs. Joanne Khanna was heard to say to her husband, 'What's the matter, darling, you keep staring at your feet. I have been watching you for the last two days and you've done nothing but stared at your feet.'

Since then a lot of people have been heard to say that. To a psychiatrist Dr. Khanna has confided that he has periods of great burning in his feet. He has further indicated that he thinks he has been cursed. [1] Dr. Khanna's output of research since he came back has been zero. He has generally come to be known as the man who does nothing but stare at his feet.

'Dr. Khana has confided that he has periods of great burning in his feet.'

1. *cursed* : put under an evil spell.

Rickshaw puller, Calcutta.

Characters

1. Dr Khanna is represented in three stages:

   i. in terms of his professional reputation;
   ii. during his meeting with the old man;
   iii. after his return to America.

   Mark the beginning and the end of each of these stages in the text and note down how he is portrayed in each stage. How can you explain the transformations he undergoes?

2. The *ashtamp farosh* is presented almost entirely through his long account of Dr Khanna's father. What can be learned, subtextually, about the *ashtamp farosh* himself?

3. Is Dr Khanna's father a character in the story? Give reasons for your answer.

Setting

The encounter between Dr Khanna and the *ashtamp farosh* takes place after a public lecture at a college in their home town. Would the effect be significantly different if they had met by chance in the street or in a private house? Why did the *ashtamp farosh* go to the lecture?

Structure

1. Read the opening paragraph again. What expectations does it arouse? Now look at the last paragraph. How is it structurally linked to the beginning of the story?

2. The *ashtamp farosh's* account of Dr Khanna's father is hardly interrupted and occupies more than half the story, forcing Dr Khanna into a largely passive role. Is this convincing? What does it suggest about Dr Khanna's relationship to his native environment?

Symbolism

Explain the importance given to feet and shoes in this story. What do you think they symbolise? Why does Dr. Khanna stare at his feet on his return to America?

Language

1. A number of words from an Indian language are used, without explanation, in the story. From the context, can you work out their probable meaning?

    i.   an *ashtamp farosh* is . . .
    ii. A *bidi* is . . .
    iii. A *cho* is . . .
    iv. *Dhak* is . . .

2. Find at least five terms in the first part of the story which show that Dr. Khanna has a strong position in the community. At what point does the writer begin to use less positive terms about him? What causes the change?

3. The *ashtamp farosh* is represented as speaking in short sentences with very little subordination. Can you think of a reason for this?

Narrator

The narrator of this story seems to be:

i.   impartial;
ii. sympathetic to Dr. Khanna;
iii. sympathetic to the *ashtamp farosh*.

Justify your choice.

Themes

1. Dr. Khanna's father believed that it was an honour for an
    Indian to be 'the only American from our village'. Why
    should he think so? What is your view?

2. The Fourth Commandment is 'Honour your father and your
    mother'. Why has Dr Khanna failed to honour his father?
    Can his conduct be justified? Do sons and daughters have
    the right to cut family ties in order to make a life of their
    own?

A Horse And Two Goats

R.K. Narayan

R. K. Narayan
(Rasipuram Krishnaswami Narayan) 1906-

Born and brought up in Madras, Narayan was not a good student and graduated from University at the relatively late age of 24. His extended family supported him, making it unnecessary for him to find a job, so he was able to concentrate on his one love, literature, reading extensively and beginning his writing career with a little journalism. He was to become internationally known and has won many awards, as well as being the only Indian writer to be made a Fellow of the American Academy and Institute of Arts and Letters – a remarkable honour.

His first novels were autobiographical and introduced the invented town of Malgudi, which was to be represented in increasing detail in later books. He has continued to use his personal experiences and acquaintances as the starting point for his fiction, which explores the conflict in Indian society between tradition and myth on the one hand, and the rationalist modern world on the other. In his many novels and short stories he has often presented serious themes like this through the medium of comedy: *A Horse And Two Goats*, first published in 1970, is an excellent example.

THE VILLAGE WAS SO SMALL that it found no mention in any atlas. On the local survey map it was indicated by a tiny dot. It was called Kiritam, which in the Tamil language means 'crown' (preferably diamond-studded)[1] – a rather gorgeous conception, readily explained by any local enthusiast convinced beyond doubt that this part of India is the apex of the world. In proof thereof,[2] he could, until quite recently, point in the direction of a massive guardian at the portals of the village, in the shape of a horse moulded out of clay, baked, burnt, and brightly coloured. The horse reared his head proudly, prancing, with his forelegs in the air and his tail looped up with a flourish.[3] Beside the horse stood a warrior with scythe-like[4] moustaches, bulging[5] eyes, and an aquiline nose. The image-makers of old had made the eyes bulge out when they wished to indicate a man of strength, just as the beads around the warrior's neck were meant to show his wealth. Blobs of mud now, before the ravages of sun and rain they had had the sparkle of emerald, ruby, and diamond. The big horse looked mottled,[6] but at one time it was white as a

---

1. *diamond-studded* : decorated with many small diamonds.
2. *thereof* : (formal, rare) of this.
3. *looped up with a flourish* : curved into a decorative ring.
4. *scythe* [sʌɪð] *-like* : like long curved blades.
5. *bulging* : protruding
6. *mottled* ['mɒtəld] : with irregular dark marks.

dhobi-washed [1] sheet, its back enveloped in a checkered brocade of pure red and black. The lance in the grip of the warrior had been covered with bands of gay colour, and the multicoloured sash [2] around his waist contrasted with every other colour in these surroundings. This statue, like scores of similar ones scattered along the countryside, was forgotten and unnoticed, with lantana [3] and cactus growing around it. Even the youthful vandals of the village left the statue alone, hardly aware of its existence. On this particular day, an old man was drowsing [4] in the shade of a nearby cactus and watching a pair of goats graze in this arid soil; he was waiting for the sight of a green bus lumbering [5] down the hill road in the evening, which would be the signal for him to start back home, and he was disturbed by a motorist, who jammed on his brakes [6] at the sight of the statue, and got out of his car, and went up to the mud horse.

'Marvellous!' he cried, pacing slowly around the statue. His face was sunburned and red. He wore a khaki-coloured shirt and shorts. Noticing the old man's presence, he said politely in English, 'How do you do?'

The old man replied in pure Tamil, his only means of communication, 'My name is Muni, and the two goats are mine and mine only; no one can gainsay [7] it, although the village is full of people ready to slander a man.'

The red-faced man rested his eyes for a moment in the direction of the goats and the rocks, took out a cigarette, and asked, 'Do you smoke?'

'I never even heard of it until yesterday,' the old man replied nervously, guessing that he was being questioned about a

1. *dhobi-washed* : washed by a professional washerwoman.
2. *sash* : belt made of cloth.
3. *lantana* : evergreen flowering bush found in India.
4. *drowsing* [drauʊzɪŋ] : sleeping lightly.
5. *lumbering* : moving heavily.
6. *jammed on his brakes* : stopped suddenly.
7. *gainsay* : contradict. This is an old-fashioned word.

murder in the neighbourhood by this police officer from the government, as his khaki dress indicated.

The red-faced man said, 'I come from New York. Have you heard of it? Have you heard of America?'

The old man would have understood the word 'America' (though not 'New York') if the name had been pronounced as he knew it – 'Ah Meh Rikya' – but the red-faced man pronounced it very differently, and the old man did not know what it meant. He said respectfully, 'Bad characters everywhere these days. The cinema has spoiled the people and taught them how to do evil things. In these days anything may happen.'

'I am sure you must know when this horse was made,' said the red-faced man, and smiled ingratiatingly.

The old man reacted to the relaxed atmosphere by smiling himself, and pleaded, 'Please go away, sir. I know nothing. I promise I will hold him for you if I see any bad character around, but our village has always had a clean record. [1] Must be the other village.'

'Please, please, I will speak slowly. Please try to understand me,' the red-faced man said. 'I arrived three weeks ago and have travelled five thousand miles since, seeing your wonderful country.'

The old man made indistinct sounds in his throat and shook his head. Encouraged by this, the other went on to explain at length, uttering each syllable with care and deliberation, what brought him to this country, how much he liked it, what he did at home, how he had planned for years to visit India, the dream of his life and so forth – every now and then pausing to smile affably. The old man smiled back and said nothing, whereupon [2] the red-faced man finally said, 'How old are you? You have such wonderful teeth. Are they real? What's your secret?'

---

1. *clean record* : good reputation.
2. *whereupon* : (formal, rare) immediately after which.

The old man knitted his brow [1] and said mournfully, 'Sometimes our cattle, too, are lost; but then we go and consult our astrologer. He will look at a camphor flame and tell us in which direction to search for the lost animals . . . I must go home now.' And he turned to go.

The other seized his shoulder and said earnestly, 'Is there no one – absolutely no one – here to translate for me?' He looked up and down the road, which was deserted on this hot afternoon. A sudden gust of wind churned up [2] the dust and the dead leaves on the roadside into a ghostly column and propelled it toward the mountain road. 'Is this statue yours? Will you sell it to me?'

The old man understood that the other was referring to the horse. He thought for a second and said, 'I was an urchin [3] of this height when I heard my grandfather explain this horse and warrior, and my grandfather himself was of this height when he heard his grandfather, whose grandfather . . .' Trying to indicate the antiquity of the statue, he got deeper and deeper into the bog of reminiscence, [4] and then pulled himself out by saying, 'But my grandfather's grandfather's uncle had first-hand knowledge, although I don't remember him.'

'Because I really do want this statue,' the red-faced man said, 'I hope you won't drive a hard bargain.'

'This horse,' the old man continued, 'will appear as the tenth avatar [5] at the end of the Yuga.' [6]

1. *knitted his brow* : frowned.

2. *churned up* : caused to move violently.

3. *urchin* : small child, usually from a poor family.

4. *the bog of reminiscence* : (fig.) distant memories which absorbed him completely.

5. *avatar* ['avətɑː]: appearance of a Hindu god in human or animal form.

6. *Yuga* : in Hindu cosmology, one of the four ages of the duration of the world.

The red-faced man nodded. He was familiar with the word 'avatar.'

'At the end of this Kali Yuga, this world will be destroyed, and all the worlds will be destroyed, and it is then that the Redeemer will come, in the form of a horse called Kalki, and help the good people, leaving the evil ones to perish in the great deluge. [1] And this horse will come to life then, and that is why this is the most sacred village in the whole world.'

'I am willing to pay any price that is reasonable –'

This statement was cut short by the old man, who was now lost in the visions of various avatars. 'God Vishnu [2] is the highest god, so our pandit [3] at the temple has always told us, and He has come nine times before, whenever evil-minded men troubled this world.'

'But please bear in mind that I am not a millionaire.'

'The first avatar was in the shape of a fish,' the old man said, and explained the story of how Vishnu at first took the form of a little fish, which grew bigger each hour and became gigantic, and supported on its back the holy scriptures, which were about to be lost in the ocean. Having launched on the first avatar, it was inevitable that he should go on with the second one, a tortoise, and the third, a boar on whose tusk the world was lifted up when it had been carried off and hidden at the bottom of the ocean by an extraordinary vicious conqueror of the earth.

'Transportation will be my problem, but I will worry about that later. Tell me, will you accept a hundred rupees for the horse only? Although I am charmed by the moustached soldier, I will have to come next year for him. No space for him now.'

'It is God Vishnu alone who saves mankind each time such a thing has happened. He incarnated himself as Rama, and He alone could destroy Ravana, the demon with ten heads who shook all the worlds. Do you know the story of Ramayana?'

---

1. *deluge* ['dɛljuːdʒ] : flood.
2. *Vishnu* : the name of a Hindu god.
3. *pandit* : (Indian) wise man.

'I have my station wagon,¹ as you see. I can push the seat
back and take the horse in. If you'll just lend me a hand with it.'

'Do you know Mahabharata? Krishna was the eighth avatar
of Vishnu, incarnated to help the Five Brothers regain their
kingdom. When Krishna was a baby, he danced on the
thousand-hooded,² the giant serpent, and trampled it to death ...'

At this stage the mutual mystification was complete. The old
man chattered away in a spirit of balancing off the credits and
debits of conversational exchanges, and said, in order to be on
the credit side, 'Oh, honourable one, I hope God has blessed you
with numerous progeny.³ I say this because you seem to be a
good man, willing to stay beside an old man and talk to him,
while all day I have none to talk to except when somebody stops
to ask for a piece of tobacco ... How many children have you?'

'Nothing ventured, nothing gained,' the red-faced man said
to himself. And then, 'Will you take a hundred rupees for it?'
Which encouraged the other to go into details.

'How many of your children are boys and how many girls?
Where are they? Is your daughter married? Is it difficult to find
a son-in-law in your country also?'

The red-faced man thrust his hand into his pocket and
brought forth his wallet, from which he took a hundred rupee
currency note.

The old man now realized that some financial element was
entering their talk. He peered closely at the currency note, the
like of which he had never seen in his life;⁴ he knew the five and
ten by their colours, although always in other people's hands.

---

1. *station wagon* : (British English estate car) car with a lot of space
   behind the back seat and an extra door at the back for loading
   and carrying large objects.

2. *the thousand-hooded* : a mythical cobra.

3. *progeny* ['prɒdʒəni]: sons and daughters.

4. *the like of which he had never seen in his life* : he had never seen
   such a valuable banknote.

His own earning at any time was in coppers and nickels. [1] What was this man flourishing [2] the note for? Perhaps for change. He laughed to himself at the notion of anyone's coming to him to change a thousand- or ten-thousand-rupee note. He said with a grin, 'Ask our village headman, who is also a money-lender; he can change even a lakh [3] of rupees in gold sovereigns if you prefer it that way. He thinks nobody knows, but dig the floor of his *puja* [4] room and your head will reel [5] at the sight of the hoard. The man disguises himself in rags just to mislead the public.'

'If that's not enough, I guess I could go a little higher,' the red-faced man said.

'You'd better talk to him yourself, because he goes mad at the sight of me. Someone took away his pumpkins with the creeper [6] and he thinks it was me and my goats. That's why I never let my goats be seen anywhere near the farms,' the old man said, with his eyes travelling to his goats as they were nosing about, attempting to wrest [7] nutrition out of minute [8] greenery peeping out of rock and dry earth.

The red-faced man followed his look and decided it would be a sound policy to show an interest in the old man's pets. He went up to them casually and stroked their backs.

Now the truth dawned on the old man. His dream of a lifetime was about to be realized: the red-faced man was making him an offer for the goats. He had reared them up in the hope of selling them some day and with the capital opening a small

1. *coppers and nickels* : coins of small value.
2. *flourishing* : waving about.
3. *lakh* [lak] : (Indian) one hundred thousand.
4. *puja* : room where Hindu gods are worshipped.
5. *reel* : go round and round.
6. *creeper* : plant which grows up walls or trees, or along the ground.
7. *wrest* : obtain with difficulty.
8. *minute* [maɪˈnjuːt] : very small.

shop on this very spot; under a thatched roof he would spread out a gunny sack [1] and display on it fried nuts, coloured sweets, and green coconut for thirsty and hungry wayfarers [2] on the highway. He needed for this project a capital of twenty rupees, and he felt that with some bargaining he could get it now; they were not prize animals worthy of a cattle show, but he had spent his occasional savings to provide them some fancy diet now and then, and they did not look too bad.

Saying, 'It is all for you, or you may share it if you have a partner,' the red-faced man placed on the old man's palm one hundred and twenty rupees in notes.

The old man pointed at the station wagon.

'Yes, of course,' said the other.

The old man said, 'This will be their first ride in a motor car. Carry them off after I get out of sight; otherwise they will never follow you but only me, even if I am travelling on the path to the Underworld.' He laughed at his own joke, brought his palms together in a salute, turned round, and was off and out of sight beyond a clump of bushes.

The red-faced man looked at the goats grazing peacefully and then perched himself on the pedestal of the horse, as the westerly sun touched off the ancient faded colours of the statue with a fresh splendour. 'He must be gone to fetch some help,' he remarked, and settled down to wait.

1. *gunny sack* : large bag made of heavy cloth, used to store food, etc.
2. *wayfarers* : travellers.

*'The red-faced man placed on the old man's palm
one hundred and twenty rupees in notes.'*

Characters

1. Choose at least two of the following adjectives to describe the men in this story. Can any of them be applied to both men?

> agitated   arrogant   bad-tempered
> considerate   gentle   imperious
> naive   optimistic   polite   stupid

2. Who is at a greater disadvantage, the American or the old man? Why?

Setting

1. Why is the statue described at such length? What is significant about the context in which it is found?

2. Read P. B. Shelley's sonnet 'Ozymandias' (printed below). In what ways does it remind you of this story?

OZYMANDIAS

I met a traveller from an antique land
Who said: Two vast and trunkless legs of stone
Stand in the desert. Near them, on the sand,
Half sunk, a shatter'd visage lies, whose frown
And wrinkled lip and sneer of cold command
Tell that its sculptor well those passions read
Which yet survive, stamp'd on these lifeless things,
The hand that mock'd them and the heart that fed.
And on the pedestal these words appear:
'My name is Ozymandias, king of kings:
Look on my works, ye mighty, and despair!'
Nothing beside remains. Round the decay
Of that colossal wreck, boundless and bare,
The lone and level sands stretch far away.

Structure

1. The story is divided into two distinct parts. Summarise the content of each part, using the prompts below.

    First part : What does the American tourist see? Who does he speak to? What does the old man think the American wants at first? What aspect of the statue does he try to explain to the American?

    Second part : What two actions on the part of the American make the old man believe he wants to buy the goats? At this point, what does the old man do?

2. There is no conventional ending to the story. Do you find this effective? What is going to happen next? Is any other development possible?

Symbolism

1. Read the description of the statue again. What aspects of Indian culture does it represent?

2. Narayan writes of the old man that he had never seen a hundred rupee note before meeting the American. Is there a sense in which the American is nevertheless poorer than the old man?

Language

1. Although the story is entirely in English, the two characters are actually speaking different languages. What stylistic device does the writer use to make this clear? (Look at vocabulary and sentence structure.)

2. List the adverbs used with verbs of speech (e.g. said, cried, replied). Do you think they are necessary? Can the reader understand how the two men are feeling without these adverbs?

3. Explain 'He got deeper and deeper into the bog of reminiscence' (p. 138). Is this an appropriate metaphor for the old man's memories, in your view? Give your reasons.

Narrator

1. Which of the following is the most accurate description of the story?

    i. It is told by an omniscient narrator.

    ii. It is told in the third person from the point of view of one of the characters.

    iii. It is told in the first person.

2. How does the choice of narrator increase the humour of the story?

Themes

1. Write a short essay on difficulties of communication between cultures. Is language the only factor that leads to the misunderstanding between the two men?

2. Look again at the title. Why did the author choose to call his story *A Horse And Two Goats*? What difference, if any, would it have made if he had called it *A Statue*?

Good Advice
Is Rarer Than Rubies

SALMAN RUSHDIE

Salman Rushdie 1947-

Born in Bombay in a Muslim family, Rushdie attended secondary school in England before going to Cambridge University, where he graduated in history; he has lived in England since 1961. His novels and short stories are characterised by recurrent themes such as the difficulties of immigrant life in Great Britain, and the conflict between good and evil. He often uses satire and broad, robust humour to make his point: this was the cause of a violent reaction in the Muslim world against his 1988 novel *The Satanic Verses*, in which, albeit indirectly, he satirises Islamic fundamentalism. As a result, he was sentenced to death by the fundamentalist leader, the Ayatollah Khomeini, and has ever since been forced to live in hiding. This has highlighted the enormous difference between Rushdie's native and adopted cultures.

O N THE LAST TUESDAY OF the month, the dawn bus, its headlamps still shining, brought Miss Rehana to the gates of the British Consulate. It arrived pushing a cloud of dust, veiling her beauty from the eyes of strangers until she descended. The bus was brightly painted in multicoloured arabesques, [1] and on the front it said 'MOVE OVER DARLING' in green and gold letters; on the back it added 'TATA-BATA' [2] and also 'O.K. GOOD-LIFE'. Miss Rehana told the driver it was a beautiful bus, and he jumped down and held the door open for her, bowing theatrically as she descended.

Miss Rehana's eyes were large and black and bright enough not to need the help of antimony, [3] and when the advice expert Muhammad Ali saw them he felt himself becoming young again. He watched her approaching the Consulate gates as the light strengthened, and asking the bearded lala who guarded them in a goldbuttoned khaki uniform with a cockaded [4] turban when they would open. The lala, usually so rude to the

---

1. *arabesques* [ærə'bɛsks] : flowing patterns.
2. *tata-bata* : meaningless graffiti.
3. *antimony* ['æntɪməni] : a powder used by Indian women to colour their eyelids.
4. *cockaded* : decorated with a knot of material.

Consulate's Tuesday women, answered Miss Rehana with something like courtesy.

'Half an hour,' he said gruffly. 'Maybe two hours. Who knows? The sahibs [1] are eating their breakfast.'

The dusty compound [2] between the bus stop and the Consulate was already full of Tuesday women, some veiled, a few barefaced like Miss Rehana. They all looked frightened, and leaned heavily on the arms of uncles or brothers, who were trying to look confident. But Miss Rehana had come on her own, and did not seem at all alarmed.

Muhammad Ali, who specialised in advising the most vulnerable-looking of these weekly supplicants, found his feet leading him towards the strange, big-eyed, independent girl.

'Miss,' he began. 'You have come for permit to London, I think so?'

She was standing at a hot-snack stall in the little shanty-town [3] by the edge of the compound, munching chilli-pakoras [4] contentedly. She turned to look at him, and at close range those eyes did bad things to his digestive tract.

'Yes, I have.'

'Then, please, you allow me to give some advice? Small cost only.'

Miss Rehana smiled. 'Good advice is rarer than rubies,' she said. 'But alas, I cannot pay. I am an orphan, not one of your wealthy ladies.'

'Trust my grey hairs,' Muhammad Ali urged her. 'My advice is well tempered by experience. You will certainly find it good.'

---

1. *sahibs* [sɑːbz] : title of respect for Europeans.
2. *compound* : enclosed area containing a group of buildings.
3. *shanty-town* : group of very poor houses made of tin or cardboard.
4. *chilli-pakoras* : spicy pancakes.

She shook her head. 'I tell you I am a poor potato. There are women here with male family members, all earning good wages. Go to them. Good advice should find good money.'

I am going crazy, Muhammad Ali thought, because he heard his voice telling her of its own volition, 'Miss, I have been drawn to you by Fate. What to do? Our meeting was written. [1] I also am a poor man only, but for you my advice comes free.'

She smiled again. 'Then I must surely listen. When Fate sends a gift, one receives good fortune.'

He led her to the low wooden desk in his own special corner of the shanty-town. She followed, continuing to eat pakoras from a little newspaper packet. She did not offer him any.

Muhammad Ali put a cushion on the dusty ground. 'Please to sit.' She did as he asked. He sat cross-legged across the desk from her, conscious that two or three dozen pairs of male eyes were watching him enviously, that all the other shanty-town men were ogling [2] the latest young lovely to be charmed by the old grey-hair fraud. He took a deep breath to settle himself.

'Name, please.'

'Miss Rehana,' she told him. 'Fiancée of Mustafa Dar of Bradford, London.'

'Bradford, England,' he corrected her gently. 'London is a town only, like Multan or Bahawalpur. [3] England is a great nation full of the coldest fish in the world.'

'I see. Thank you,' she responded gravely, so that he was unsure if she was making fun of him.

'You have filled application form? Then let me see, please.'

She passed him a neatly folded document in a brown envelope.

'Is it OK?' For the first time there was a note of anxiety in her voice.

1. *Our meeting was written* : it was destined to happen.
2. *ogling* : looking with sexual interest.
3. *Multan or Bahawalpur* : towns in East Pakistan.

He patted the desk quite near the place where her hand rested. 'I am certain,' he said. 'Wait on and I will check.'

She finished the pakoras while he scanned her papers.

'Tip-top,' [1] he pronounced at length. 'All in order.'

'Thank you for your advice,' she said, making as if to rise. 'I'll go now and wait by the gate.'

'What are you thinking?' he cried loudly, smiting [2] his forehead. 'You consider this is easy business? Just give the form and poof, with a big smile they hand over the permit? Miss Rehana, I tell you, you are entering a worse place than any police station.'

'Is it so, truly?' His oratory had done the trick. She was a captive audience now, and he would be able to look at her for a few moments longer.

Drawing another calming breath, he launched into his set speech. [3] He told her that the sahibs thought that all the women who came on Tuesdays, claiming to be dependents of bus drivers in Luton [4] or chartered accountants in Manchester, were crooks [5] and liars and cheats.

She protested, 'But then I will simply tell them that I, for one, am no such thing!'

Her innocence made him shiver with fear for her. She was a sparrow, he told her, and they were men with hooded [6] eyes, like hawks. He explained that they would ask her questions, personal questions, questions such as a lady's own brother would be too shy to ask. They would ask if she was virgin, and,

---

1. *tip-top* : perfect. This is a very old-fashioned slang expression.
2. *smiting* : hitting.
3. *set speech* : speech which has been prepared and often repeated.
4. *Luton* : town in the south of England.
5. *crooks* : criminals.
6. *hooded* : (here) with the lids lowered.

if not, what her fiancé's love-making habits were, and what secret nicknames they had invented for one another.

Muhammad Ali spoke brutally, on purpose, to lessen the shock she would feel when it, or something like it, actually happened. Her eyes remained steady, but her hands began to flutter at the edges of the desk.

He went on:

'They will ask you how many rooms are in your family home, and what colour are the walls, and what days do you empty the rubbish. They will ask your man's mother's third cousin's aunt's step-daughter's [1] middle name. And all these things they have already asked your Mustafa Dar in his Bradford. And if you make one mistake, you are finished.'

'Yes,' she said, and he could hear her disciplining her voice. 'And what is your advice, old man?'

It was at this point that Muhammad Ali usually began to whisper urgently, to mention that he knew a man, a very good type, who worked in the Consulate, and through him, for a fee, the necessary papers could be delivered, with all the proper authenticating seals. Business was good, because the women would often pay him five hundred rupees or give him a gold bracelet for his pains, and go away happy.

They came from hundreds of miles away – he normally made sure of this before beginning to trick them – so even when they discovered they had been swindled [2] they were unlikely to return. They went away to Sargodha or Lalukhet and began to pack, and who knows at what point they found out they had been gulled, [3] but it was at a too-late point, anyway.

---

1. *step-daughter* : daughter of the aunt's husband's previous marriage.
2. *swindled* : treated dishonestly.
3. *gulled* [gʌld] : deceived.

Life is hard, and an old man must live by his wits. [1] It was not up to Muhammad Ali to have compassion for these Tuesday women.

But once again his voice betrayed him, and instead of starting his customary speech it began to reveal to her his greatest secret.

'Miss Rehana,' his voice said, and he listened to it in amazement, 'you are a rare person, a jewel, and for you I will do what I would not do for my own daughter, perhaps. One document has come into my possession that can solve all your worries at one stroke.'

'And what is this sorcerer's paper?' she asked, her eyes unquestionably laughing at him now.

His voice fell low-as-low.

'Miss Rehana, it is a British passport. Completely genuine and pukka goods. I have a good friend who will put your name and photo, and then, hey-presto, [2] England there you come!'

He had said it!

Anything was possible now, on this day of his insanity. Probably he would give her the thing free-gratis, and then kick himself for a year afterwards.

Old fool, he berated [3] himself. *The oldest fools are bewitched by the youngest girls.*

'Let me understand you,' she was saying. 'You are proposing I should commit a crime . . .'

'Not crime,' he interposed. 'Facilitation.'

'. . . and go to Bradford, London, illegally, and therefore

---

1. *live by his wits* : survive by using his intelligence, without a regular job.

2. *hey-presto* : (used by magicians) here is the result of the trick!

3. *berated* : spoke angrily to.

justify the low opinion the Consulate sahibs have of us all. Old babuji,[1] this is not good advice.'

'Bradford, *England*,' he corrected her mournfully. 'You should not take my gift in such a spirit.'

'Then how?'

'Bibi,[2] I am a poor fellow, and I have offered this prize because you are so beautiful. Do not spit on my generosity. Take the thing. Or else don't take, go home, forget England, only do not go into that building and lose your dignity.'

But she was on her feet, turning away from him, walking towards the gates, where the women had begun to cluster and the lala was swearing at them to be patient or none of them would be admitted at all.

'So be a fool,' Muhammad Ali shouted after her. 'What goes of my father's if you are?' (Meaning, what was it to him.)[3]

She did not turn.

'It is the curse of our people,' he yelled. 'We are poor, we are ignorant, and we completely refuse to learn.'

'Hey, Muhammad Ali,' the woman at the betel-nut stall called across to him. 'Too bad, she likes them young.'

That day Muhammad Ali did nothing but stand around near the Consulate gates. Many times he scolded himself, *Go from here, old goof, lady does not desire to speak with you any further.* But when she came out, she found him waiting.

'Salaam, advice wallah,'[4] she greeted him.

She seemed calm, and at peace with him again, and he thought, *My God, ya Allah, she has pulled it off. The British sahibs also have been drowning in her eyes and she has got her passage to England.*

---

1. *babuji* : (Hindustani) form of address to a gentleman.
2. *bibi* : (Hindustani) lady.
3. *what was it to him* : what did it matter to him.
4. *wallah* : man with a specific job.

He smiled at her hopefully. She smiled back with no trouble at all.

'Miss Rehana Begum,' he said, 'felicitations, daughter, on what is obviously your hour of triumph.'

Impulsively, she took his forearm in her hand.

'Come,' she said. 'Let me buy you a pakora to thank you for your advice and to apologise for my rudeness, too.'

They stood in the dust of the afternoon compound near the bus, which was getting ready to leave. Coolies [1] were tying bedding rolls [2] to the roof. A hawker [3] shouted at the passengers, trying to sell them love stories and green medicines, both of which cured unhappiness. Miss Rehana and a happy Muhammad Ali ate their pakoras sitting on the bus's 'front mud-guard', that is, the bumper. [4] The old advice expert began softly to hum a tune from a movie soundtrack. The day's heat was gone.

'It was an arranged engagement,' Miss Rehana said all at once. 'I was nine years old when my parents fixed it. Mustafa Dar was already thirty at that time, but my father wanted someone who could look after me as he had done himself and Mustafa was a man known to Daddyji as a solid type. Then my parents died and Mustafa Dar went to England and said he would send for me. That was many years ago. I have his photo, but he is like a stranger to me. Even his voice, I do not recognise it on the phone.'

The confession took Muhammad Ali by surprise, but he nodded with what he hoped looked like wisdom.

---

1. *coolies* : low-paid workers.
2. *bedding rolls* : light mattresses.
3. *hawker* : street vendor.
4. *bumper* : metal bar on the front and back of vehicle to protect it in a collision.

'Still and after all,' he said, 'one's parents act in one's best interests. They found you a good and honest man who has kept his word and sent for you. And now you have a lifetime to get to know him, and to love.'

He was puzzled, now, by the bitterness that had infected her smile.

'But, old man,' she asked him, 'why have you already packed me and posted me off to England?'

He stood up, shocked.

'You looked happy – so I just assumed . . . excuse me, but they turned you down or what?'

'I got all their questions wrong,' she replied. 'Distinguishing marks I put on the wrong cheeks, bathroom decor I completely redecorated, all absolutely topsy-turvy, [1] you see.'

'But what to do? How will you go?'

'Now I will go back to Lahore and my job. I work in a great house, as ayah [2] to three good boys. They would have been sad to see me leave.'

'But this is tragedy!' Muhammad Ali lamented. 'Oh, how I pray that you had taken up my offer! Now, but, it is not possible, I regret to inform. Now they have your form on file, cross-check [3] can be made, even the passport will not suffice.

'It is spoilt, all spoilt, and it could have been so easy if advice had been accepted in good time.'

'I do not think,' she told him, 'I truly do not think you should be sad.'

Her last smile, which he watched from the compound until the bus concealed it in a dust-cloud, was the happiest thing he had ever seen in his long, hot, hard, unloving life.

---

1. *topsy-turvy* : in great disorder.
2. *ayah* ['æɪə] : (Indian) nurse who looks after children.
3. *cross-check* : very careful check of correctness.

'Her last smile . . . was the happiest thing
he had ever seen in his long, hot, hard unloving life.

Characters

1. How does Rushdie show, in the first two or three pages of the story, that Miss Rehana is a kind, thoughtful, polite young woman?

2. What evidence is there of her fundamental naivety?

3. Do you think Muhammad Ali's attitude towards her is fatherly, or is he motivated by sexual attraction? Quote from the story to support your answer.

4. Which of the two is the main character, in your opinion? Give reasons for your answer.

Setting

Make a list of the elements in the description of the setting which are clearly non-European. What social level do they seem to indicate?

Structure

The story is divided into fourteen brief sections. Is this effective? On what basis are the sections separated from each other? How would the narrative be altered if the story were printed as a continuous whole?

Language

1. Miss Rehana and Muhammad Ali address each other with various titles. List these and decide which of them are the most formal.

2. As in a number of stories in this volume, the dialogue here is characterised by non-standard grammar. Identify at least five examples. Are these non-standard forms the same as you have found in other stories?

3. Attempt a definition of the following expressions, using the context to help you:

   i. a poor potato (p. 151);

   ii. the coldest fish in the world (p. 151)

   iii. pukka goods (p. 154);

   iv. old goof (p. 155);

   v. a solid type (p. 156).

Narrator

Rushdie gives the reader some information about Muhammad Ali which Miss Rehana does not know about him. Find examples. Would your attitude to Muhammad Ali be the same if you were in Miss Rehana's position?

Themes

1. What advantages and disadvantages of arranged marriages are suggested by the story? In your view, are there circumstances in which an arranged marriage might be desirable?

2. The title of this story is a quotation from the Song of Songs, one of the books of the Old Testament, and is spoken by Miss Rehana in the course of her conversation with Muhammad Ali. Do you find it an effective title? In what sense is it ironic?

New Zealand

The Hole That Jack Dug

FRANK SARGESON

Frank Sargeson 1903-82

After training as a solicitor and visiting Europe, Frank Sargeson abandoned his job and his home, going to live in a hut by the sea in a suburb of Auckland, where he later built a small house: this was his home for the rest of his life. There he dedicated himself to writing, concentrating on simple, uneducated people and using the colloquial speech patterns of the working classes to explore their humanity at a much deeper level than their surface simplicity might suggest: in this he was influenced by the Australian Henry Lawson and by the American Sherwood Anderson. In addition to several novels and a collection of short stories, Sargeson – whose real name was Norris Frank Davey – wrote three volumes of autobiography, in which he portrays the sectors of society in which he had chosen to live. He also gave generous encouragement to young writers.

JACK HAD GOT A PRETTY considerable hole dug in the backyard before I knew anything about it. I went around one scorching hot Saturday afternoon, and Jack was in the hole with nothing on except his boots and his little tight pair of shorts. Jack is a big specimen of a bloke, [1] he's very powerfully developed, and seeing he's worked in the quarry for years in just that rigout, [2] he's browned a darker colour than you'd ever believe possible on a white man. And that afternoon he was sweating so much he had a shine on as well.

'Hello Jack,' I said, 'doing a spot of work?' [3]

And Jack leaned on his shovel and grinned up at me. The trouble with Jack's grin is that it shows too many teeth. It's easy to pick they're not the real thing, [4] and I've always thought they somehow don't fit in with the rest of him. Also his eyes are sky-blue, and it almost scares you to see them staring out of all that sunburn. I don't say they don't fit in though. They always have a bit of a crazy look about them, and even though Jack is my closest cobber [5] I will say that he'll do some crazy things.

1. *bloke* : (informal) man.
2. *rigout* : a set of clothes worn at the same time. This word usually has negative connotations.
3. *a spot of work* : a little work.
4. *it's easy to pick they're not the real thing* : they are obviously artificial.
5. *cobber* : (Australian slang) friend (used of men by men).

'Yes Tom,' he said, 'I'm doing a job.'

'But it's hot work,' I said.

I've said it was scorching hot and it was. We'd been having a good summer, the first one after the war broke out. You'd hear folks say what lovely days we were having, and you'd be somehow always telling yourself you just couldn't believe there was any war on, when everything round about you looked so fine and dandy. [1] But anyhow, I was just going to ask Jack if he wanted a hand, when his missis [2] opened the back door and asked if I'd go in and have a cup of tea.

'No thanks, Mrs Parker,' I said, 'I've only just had one.'

She didn't ask Jack, but he said he could do with one, so we both went inside and his missis had several of her friends there. She always has stacks [3] of friends, and most times you'll find them around. But I'm Jack's friend, about the only one he has that goes to the house. I first ran across Jack in camp during the last war, though I only got to be cobbers with him a fair while after, [4] when we lived at the same boardinghouse and worked at the same job, shovelling cement. In those days he hadn't started to trot the sheila he eventually married, though later on when he did I heard all about it. It knocked Jack over [5] properly. He was always telling me about how she was far too good for him, a girl with her brains and refinement. Before she came out from England she'd been a governess, and I remember how Jack said she'd read more than ten books by an author called Hugh Walpole. Anyhow Jack was knocked over properly, and I reckon she must have been too. Or why did she marry him? As for me, I reckon it was because she did have the brains to tell a real man when she saw one, and hook on to him [6] when she got the

---

1. *fine and dandy* : (informal) pleasant, free of problems.
2. *missis* : (informal) wife.
3. *stacks* : (informal) lots.
4. *a fair while after* : considerably later.
5. *it knocked Jack over* : (informal) it amazed Jack.
6. *hook on to him* : (informal) catch him like a fish.

chance. But all that must be well over twenty years ago now, and it's always a wonder to me the way Jack still thinks his missis is the greatest kid that ever was, even though she couldn't make it plainer than she does, without a word said, that she's changed her mind about him. Not that you can altogether blame her of course. Just about any man, I should say, would find it awfully trying [1] to be a woman married to Jack. But for a cobber you couldn't pick on a finer bloke.

One thing Mrs Parker's always had against Jack is that he's stayed working in the quarry year after year, instead of trying to get himself a better job. Meaning by a better job one that brings in more pay, without it mattering if it's only senseless and stupid sort of work you have to do. Of course, Jack knows that to run the house, with the snooks growing up fast, his missis could have always done with considerably more money than he's able to let her have. He lets her have the lot anyway, he never would smoke or drink or put money on a horse. [2] But he isn't the sort that's got much show of ever being in the big money, and any case it would need to be pretty big, because his missis is always coming to light with some big ideas. Not to mention a car, one thing she's always on about is a refrigerator. It would save money in the long run is what she reckons, and maybe she's right, but it's always seemed too much of a hurdle [3] to Jack.

'Do you know dear,' I heard him say once, 'when I was a little boy, and my mother opened the safe, [4] and there was a blowfly [5] buzzing about, it sometimes wouldn't even bother to fly inside.'

And Mrs Parker said, 'What's a blowfly (or your mother for that matter) got to do with us having a refrigerator?' And Jack went on grinning until she got cross and said, 'Well, why wouldn't it fly inside?'

---

1. *trying* : difficult, irritating.
2. *put money on a horse* : risk money on the result of a horse race.
3. *hurdle* ['hɜːdəl] : obstacle.
4. *safe* : (here) cupboard for food.
5. *blowfly* : kind of fly which puts its eggs on meat.

'Because dear,' Jack said, 'it knew it was no good flying inside.'

And you could tell it annoyed his missis because she still couldn't work it out, but she wasn't going to let on [1] by asking Jack to explain.

But I was telling about that Saturday afternoon when we went inside, and Jack had his cup of tea and I wouldn't have one.

'Well, do sit down,' Mrs Parker said to me, but I stayed standing. It sounds dirty I know, but I'd had years of experience behind me. I've only got a sort of polite interest in Jack's missis and those friends of hers. They're always talking about books and writers, but never any I know anything about. Henry Lawson now, that would be different. Though I've always remembered that name Hugh Walpole, and once I started one of his, I forget the name, but I never got past the first chapter. I only go there because I'm Jack's cobber, but Mrs Parker is a mighty good-looking woman, so I suppose she's always naturally expected everybody of the male sex to be more interested in her than in her old man. Everybody is anyhow, except me. But still she's never seemed satisfied. And with things that way I've usually always picked on fine weekends to go round and see Jack, because then the pair of us can work in the garden, and I don't have to listen to his missis all the time nipping at him. And times when it comes on wet I've usually shoved off, [2] though sometimes we've gone and sat yarning [3] on the camp stretcher in the little room off the back verandah where Jack sleeps. Jack mightn't have the brains that his missis has but he isn't dumb, and I've always liked to hear him talk. He's such a good-natured cuss, [4] always wanting everything in

1. *let on* : reveal her secret.
2. *shoved off* : (informal) gone away.
3. *yarning* : (informal) chatting.
4. *cuss* : (slang) man.

the garden to be lovely [1] for everybody that walks the earth, and he'll spout [2] little pieces of poetry to show what he means. Years before the war broke out I was listening to him talking about the way things were going with the world, and saying what he thought was going to happen. After all, the pair of us had been in the last war, and I agreed when Jack said he could see it all coming again. And he had more to worry about than I had, because his eldest one was a colt. (I say was, because later on it was rotten [3] to get the news from Italy about him.)

Anyhow, one reason I stayed standing when Mrs Parker asked me to sit down, was because I thought I'd get Jack back into the garden sooner if I didn't sit down. And although he grinned round at the company, looking awfully hairy and sweaty though not too naked on account of his dark colour, and even spouted one of his pieces of poetry (which his missis several times tried to interrupt), he was all the time gulping several cups of tea down hot, and I reckoned he had that hole he was digging on his mind, which as it turned out he had.

That hole!

It was right up against the wash-house wall, and we went out and looked at it, and Jack said it would take a lot of work but never mind. He said he hadn't thought about me giving him a hand, but never mind that either. We could widen it another four feet so the pair of us could work there together. And he went and got the spade, and I began by taking the turf off the extra four feet, while Jack got down below again with the shovel.

Now I've known Jack a longer time than his missis has, so maybe that's the reason why I know it's never any good pestering him with straightout [4] questions, because if you do

---

1. *everything in the garden to be lovely* : from the common expression everything in the garden's lovely, all is well.
2. *spout* : (slang) recite.
3. *rotten* : (informal) very sad.
4. *straightout* : direct. Straight out is often used as an adverb ('I asked him straight out if he had taken my pen').

you only get an answer back like the one I'd heard his missis get over the refrigerator. Only seeing Jack knows me pretty thoroughly, he'll probably make it a lot more difficult to work out than that one was. So if he wanted to dig a hole that was all right with me, and I thought if I just kept my mouth shut I'd find out in plenty of good time what he was digging it for. To begin with though, I don't know that I thought about it much at all. It was Jack's concern, and he didn't have to tell me.

But I admit it wasn't long before I began wondering. You see, when we finished up that Saturday afternoon Jack said we'd done a good job of work, but how about if I came round and we carried on one night during the week? And that was all right, I said for one night I could cut out taking a few bob off the lads [1] that were learning to play billiards along at the room, and I'd make it Wednesday. And Wednesday after work I had my wash but didn't change out of my working clothes, and after dinner I got on my bike and went round to Jack's place and found him hard at it. Also it was easy to tell this wasn't the only night he'd been working because already by now it was a whopping great [2] hole he was working in. Anyhow we had our usual yarn, then the pair of us got to work and kept on until it was too dark to see any more. And just about then Jack's missis came round the corner of the wash-house.

'Whatever are you two boys doing?' she wanted to know.

'We've been working Mrs Parker,' I said.

'Yes,' she said, 'but what are you digging that hole for?'

'You see dear,' Jack said, 'some people say they don't like work, but what would we ever have if we didn't work? And now the war's on we've all got to do our share. Think of the soldier-boys. Fighting's hard work, and Tom and me want to do our bit as well.'

---

1. *cut out taking a few bob off the lads* : (informal) Tom was willing to miss his usual game of billiards, where he always won small sums of money from the other men. A bob is slang for a shilling (old currency).

2. *whopping great* : (slang) enormous.

But before he'd finished Mrs Parker had gone inside again. I
was putting my bicycle clips on my trousers, but Jack was still
down the hole, and he asked if I'd mind handing him down a
box with a candle and matches that I'd see in the wash-house. I
watched while he lit up and fixed the box so the light shone
where he wanted to work. And for a few minutes I stayed
watching, the shovel going in deep each time under his weight,
the candle-light showing up the hollows and curves made by his
big muscles, and the sweat making him look as if he was all
covered with oil. I left him to it, but said I'd be round again
Saturday afternoon, and going home I thought perhaps it was a
septic tank he was putting in. Or was it an asparagus bed? or
was he going to set a grape vine? It was evidently going to be a
proper job any way, whatever it was.

Well. The job went on for weeks. As far as I could make out
Jack must have come home and worked at it every night until
late. He didn't like taking time off to shift away the spoil [1] from
the edge, so that was the job I took on, and I must have shifted
tons of the stuff down to the bottom of the garden in the
wheelbarrow. Nor would Jack let me go down the hole any
more, he said it was too dangerous, and it certainly looked like
it. Because once he'd got down deep he started to under-cut in
all directions, particularly on the wash-house side, which
seemed pretty crazy to me. Once he struck rock, so brought
some gelly [2] home from the quarry and plugged a bit in and set
it off, [3] and it brought a lot of earth down on the wash-house
side. Then he had to get to work and spend a lot of time rigging
up props [4] in case the blocks that were holding the wash-house
up came through. I was hanged if I could get a line on [5] what it

---

1. *spoil* : earth, stones etc. dug out of a hole.
2. *gelly* ['dʒɛli] : abbreviation of gelignite.
3. *plugged a bit in and set it off* : pushed a small quantity into the
   earth and caused it to explode.
4. *rigging up props* : fixing supports.
5. *I was hanged if I could get a line on* : I couldn't understand at all.

was all about, and it was beginning to get me worried. His missis didn't ask any more questions, not while I was there anyhow, but I noticed she was getting round with a worried look, and I'd never felt that way before but I did feel a bit sorry for her then. About the only ones that got a kick out of [1] the business were Jack's youngest snooks. The gelly he set off had been a real bit of fun for them, and they and their cobbers were always hanging around in the hope of another explosion. One that would finish off the wash-house, no doubt. Another thing was that for several weeks Jack hadn't done a tap [2] of work in the garden, and one afternoon when Mrs Parker came out with cups of tea for us, she said he must be losing his eyesight if he couldn't see there was plenty just crying out to be done. [3]

'Yes dear,' Jack said, in that good-natured sort of loving tone he always uses to her. Things being what they are between them, I can understand how it must make her want to knock him over the head. 'Yes dear,' he said, 'but just now there are other things for Tom and me to do.'

He was sitting on the edge of the hole, and after the strain of a long bout of shovelling his chest was going like a big pair of bellows worked by machinery. The day was another scorcher but blowy [4] as well, and the dust had stuck to him, and run and caked, and stuck again, until about all you could see that was actually him was those eyes of his. And the bloodshot white and pure blue staring out of all that was something you almost couldn't bear to look at.

'Yes dear,' he repeated, 'we have other things to do.'

And it was just then that half a dozen planes flying down quite low happened to suddenly come over. And of course we all of us stared up at them.

1. *got a kick out of* : got pleasure from.
2. *tap* : (informal New Zealand) very small amount.
3. *crying out to be done* : in urgent need of being done.
4. *blowy* : windy.

'You see dear,' Jack went on saying, though you could hardly hear him for the noise of the planes. 'You see dear,' he said, 'we have more important things to do than those boys flying up there. Or at any rate,' he went on, 'just as important.'

But since we were watching the planes we didn't pay much attention to him. And it wasn't until they were nearly out of sight that I realised he'd disappeared down the hole again. You could tell he was there all right. The shovelfuls of spoil were coming flying up over the edge at a tremendous rate. And it was only afterwards, thinking it over, that I remembered what he'd been saying.

Well. This is the end of my yarn about Jack and the hole he dug. Next time I went round he was filling it in again, and he'd already got a fair bit done. All he said was that if he didn't go ahead and get his winter garden in he'd be having the family short of vegetables. And his missis had told him he'd got to do something about the hole because it was dangerous when there were kids about. So I took over wheeling the stuff up from the bottom of the garden, and Jack rammed it back in so tight that by the time he was up to ground level again there was practically nothing left over.

I must end up with a joke though. It was only a few summers later we had the Jap scare, [1] and Jack earned a considerable amount of money digging shelters for people who were wanting them put in in a hurry, and weren't so particular how much they paid to get the work done. His missis appreciated the extra money, but she was always on to him to dig one for the family. All her friends agreed it was scandalous, the callous [2] way he didn't seem to care if his own wife and children were all blown to bits!

As for me, I'm ready to stick up for Jack any time. Though I don't say his missis is making a mistake when she says that some day he'll end up in the lunatic asylum.

---

1. *the Jap scare* : widespread fear of a Japanese invasion.
2. *callous* : totally insensitive.

Characters

1. Characterisation may be achieved in various ways: for example, through direct description, through dialogue, through relationships etc.

    i. What are we told directly about Jack? Quote from the text in support of your answer.

    ii. What do we learn from his conversations with his wife? Is there any special significance in the fact that he repeatedly calls her 'dear'?

    iii. How would you define the narrator's relationship with Jack? Choose one or more of the adjectives listed below.

    > casual   diffident   neutral   protective
    > suspicious   sympathetic   uncomprehending

2. Write a short description of Mrs Parker. Do you find her a likeable character? Why/Why not?

3. Read the short exchange on pp. 167-8, beginning 'Do you know, dear, I heard him say once' and ending 'by asking Jack to explain'. What is the point of Jack's story about the blowfly? Why does Mrs Parker fail to understand it?

Setting

1. Part of the story is set inside the house, part of it outside, in the garden. What is suggested about these two environments? How do they relate to the principal characters?

2. Comment on Jack's bedroom in the light of what you have said in answer to the previous question.

Structure

1. The story can be divided into seven sections. In the chart below, show where each section begins and ends. The first one has been done for you.

Section	Beginning and end
i	From 'Jack had got' to 'several of her friends there'
ii	
iii	
iv	
v	
vi	
vii	

2. What is the point of the epilogue?

3. Jack's eyes are mentioned twice in the story. At what points? What does Tom say about Jack's eyes on both occasions?

Language

1. Make a list of the colloquial elements used in Tom's narrative. What do they tell us about Tom?

2. Attempt a definition of the following expressions, using the context to help you:

    i. to trot the sheila

    ii. the snooks

    iii. a colt

    iv. nipping at him

    v. hard at it.

3. On p. 169 we read:

And he had more to worry about than I had, because his eldest one was a colt. (I say was, because later on it was rotten to get the news from Italy about him.)

What does 'one' stand for in the first sentence? What was the news from Italy?

Narrator

1. How would the story be changed if it were narrated by Mrs Parker?

2. What impression do you have of Tom's character?

Themes

1. There is a long-standing Australian tradition of the importance of friendship between men, illustrated here by Tom's loyalty to Jack. What do you think about this? Do members of the same sex understand each other better than members of opposite sexes? Should friendship be regarded as secondary to marriage?

2. Why is Mrs Parker so critical of her husband? Which of them do you sympathise with? Why is their marriage such a difficult one?

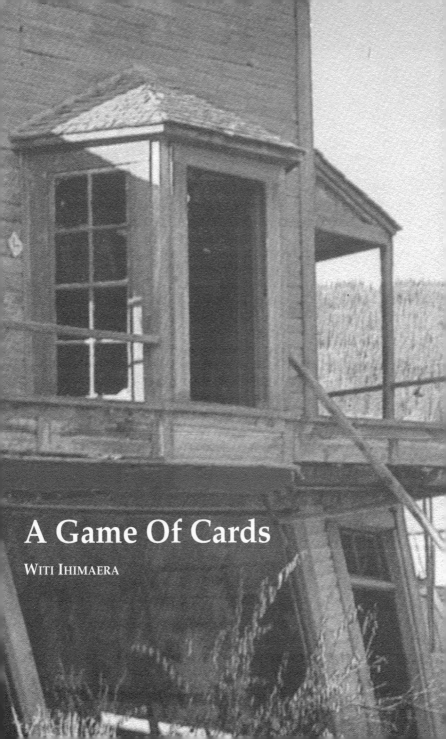

A Game Of Cards

Witi Ihimaera

Witi Ihimaera 1944-

As his name suggests, Ihimaera is of Maori descent: he was the first Maori to publish a volume of short stories and the first to publish a novel. A graduate of the Universities of Auckland and Victoria, he has worked for the New Zealand Ministry of foreign affairs, has been New Zealand Consul in New York and counsellor at the New Zealand Embassy in Washington, the American capital. This distinguished career makes him a very untypical Maori, but he has shown his loyalty to his native culture in his writings, where he contrasts the values of the Maori community with those of the Pakeha (white) community and gives prominence to the role of the whanau, the extended family characteristic of Maori society. This is clear in the story chosen for this volume, where the whole whanau participates, physically and emotionally, in the death of an old woman.

THE TRAIN PULLED INTO THE STATION. For a moment there was confusion: a voice blaring over the loudspeaker system, people getting off the train, the bustling and shoving [1] of the crowd on the platform. And there was Dad, waiting for me. We hugged each other. We hadn't seen each other for a long time. Then we kissed. But I could tell something was wrong.

'Your Nanny Miro,' he said. 'She's very sick.'

Nanny Miro . . . among all my nannies, [2] she was the one I loved most. Everybody used to say I was her favourite mokopuna, and that she loved me more than her own children who'd grown up and had kids of their own.

She lived down the road from us, right next to the meeting house in the big old homestead which everybody in the village called 'The Museum' because it housed the prized possessions of the whanau, the village family. Because she was rich and had a lot of land, we all used to wonder why Nanny Miro didn't buy a newer, more modern house. But Nanny didn't want to move. She liked her own house just as it was.

'Anyway,' she used to say, 'what with all my haddit [3] kids

---

1. *bustling and shoving* : quick, busy movement and pushing.
2. *nannies* : literally, grandmothers. The whanau, as the story explains, is an extended family, in which a child may have many 'grandmothers'.
3. *haddit* : (informal, Maori) damned.

and their haddit kids and all this haddit whanau being broke all the time and coming to ask me for some money, how can I afford to buy a new house?'

Nanny didn't really care about money though. 'Who needs it?' she used to say. 'What you think I had all these kids for, ay? To look after me, I'm not dumb!' [1]

Then she would cackle [2] to herself. But it wasn't true really, because her family would send all their kids to her place when they were broke and she looked after them! She liked her mokopunas, but not for too long. She'd ring up their parents and say:

'Hey! When you coming to pick up your hoha kids! They're wrecking the place!'

Yet, always, when they left, she would have a little weep, and give them some money . . .

I used to like going to Nanny's place. For me it was a big treasure house, glistening with sports trophies and photographs, pieces of carvings and greenstone, [3] and feather cloaks hanging from the walls.

Most times, a lot of women would be there playing cards with Nanny. Nanny loved all card games – five hundred, poker, canasta, pontoon, whist, euchre [4] – you name it, she could play it.

The sitting room would be crowded with the kuias, [5] all puffing clouds of smoke, dressed in their old clothes, laughing and cackling and gossiping about who was pregnant – and relishing all the juicy [6] bits too!

---

1. *dumb* : (informal) stupid.
2. *cackle* : laugh loudly and unmusically.
3. *greenstone* : a type of stone from volcanic material, typical of New Zealand.
4. *five hundred, poker, canasta, pontoon, whist, euchre* : card games for two or more players.
5. *kuias* : (Maori) women.
6. *juicy* : (here) interesting because rather shocking.

I liked sitting and watching them. Mrs Heta would always be there, and when it came to cards she was both Nanny's best friend and worst enemy. And the two of them were the biggest cheats I ever saw.

Mrs Heta would cough and reach for a hanky while slyly slipping a card from beneath her dress. And she was always reneging [1] in five hundred! But her greatest asset [2] was her eyes, which were big and googly. [3] One eye would look straight ahead, while the other swivelled [4] around, having a look at the cards in the hands of the women sitting next to her.

'Eeee! You cheat!' Nanny would say. 'You just keep your eyes to yourself, Maka tiko bum!'

Mrs Heta would look at Nanny as if she were offended. Then she would sniff and say:

'You the cheat yourself, Miro Mananui. I saw you sneaking that ace from the bottom of the pack.'

'How do you know I got all ace Maka?' Nanny would say. 'I know you! You dealt this hand, and you stuck that ace down there for yourself, you cheat! Well, ana! I got it now! So take that!'

And she would slap down her hand.

'Sweet, ay?' she would laugh. 'Good? Kapai lalelale?' [5] And she would sometimes wiggle her hips, making her victory sweeter.

'Eeee! Miro!' Mrs Heta would say. 'Well, I got a good hand too!'

And she would slap her hand down and bellow with laughter. 'Take that!'

1. *reneging* : breaking the rules of a card game by playing a card of the wrong suit when you have a card of the right suit in your hand.
2. *asset* : (here) attractive feature.
3. *googly* : large, round and staring.
4. *swivelled* : turned in the opposite direction.
5. *Kapai lalelale* : (Maori) very good.

And always, they would squabble. I often wondered how they ever remained friends. The names they called each other!

Sometimes, I would go and see Nanny and she would be all alone, playing patience. [1] If there was nobody to play with her, she'd always play patience. And still she cheated! I'd see her hands fumbling across the cards, turning up a jack or queen she needed, and then she'd laugh and say:

'I'm too good for this game!'

She used to try to teach me some of the games, but I wasn't very interested, and I didn't yell and shout at her like the women did. She liked the bickering.

'Aue . . .' she would sigh. Then she'd look at me and begin dealing out the cards in the only game I ever knew how to play.

And we would yell snap! [2] all the afternoon . . .

Now, Nanny was sick.

I went to see her that afternoon after I'd dropped my suitcases at home. Nanny Tama, her husband, opened the door. We embraced and he began to weep on my shoulder.

'Your Nanny Miro,' he whispered. 'She's . . . she's . . .'

He couldn't say the words. He motioned me to her bedroom.

Nanny Miro was lying in bed. And she was so old looking. Her face was very grey, and she looked like a tiny wrinkled doll in that big bed. She was so thin now, and seemed all bones.

I walked into the room. She was asleep. I sat down on the bed beside her, and looked at her lovingly.

Even when I was a child, she must have been old. But I'd never realised it. She must have been over seventy now. Why do people you love grow old so suddenly?

The room had a strange, antiseptic smell. Underneath the bed was a big chamber pot, [3] yellow with urine . . . And the

---

1. *patience* : card game for one player.
2. *snap!* : said during the game of 'snap' when a player notices that two cards of the same value have been put down.
3. *chamber pot* : round container used as a toilet by someone who is ill in bed.

pillow was flecked with small spots of blood where she had been coughing.

I shook her gently.

'Nanny . . . Nanny, wake up.'

She moaned. A long, hoarse sigh grew on her lips. Her eyelids fluttered, and she looked at me with blank eyes . . . and then tears began to roll down her cheeks.

'Don't cry, Nanny,' I said. 'Don't cry. I'm here.'

But she wouldn't stop.

So I sat beside her on the bed and she lifted her hands to me.

'Haere mai, mokopuna. Haere mai. Mmm. Mmm.'

And I bent within her arms and we pressed noses.

After a while, she calmed down. She seemed to be her own self.

'What a haddit mokopuna you are,' she wept. 'It's only when I'm just about in my grave that you come to see me.'

'I couldn't see you last time I was home,' I explained. 'I was too busy.'

'Yes, I know you fullas,'[1] she grumbled. 'It's only when I'm almost dead that you come for some money.'

'I don't want your money, Nanny.'

'What's wrong with my money!' she said. 'Nothing's wrong with it! Don't you want any?'

'Of course I do,' I laughed. 'But I know you! I bet you lost it all on poker!'

She giggled. Then she was my Nanny again. The Nanny I knew.

We talked for a long time. I told her about what I was doing in Wellington and all the neat[2] girls who were after me.

'You teka!' she giggled. 'Who'd want to have you!'

And she showed me all her injection needles and pills and

1. *fullas* : the spelling represents Nanny Miro's pronunciation of 'fellows', men.

2. *neat* : (informal, esp. US, Australia) attractive.

told me how she'd wanted to come from the hospital, so they'd let her.

'You know why I wanted to come home?' she asked. 'I didn't like all those strange nurses looking at my bum when they gave me those injections. I was so sick, mokopuna, I couldn't even go to the lav, [1] and I'd rather wet my own bed not their neat bed. That's why I come home.'

Afterwards, I played the piano for Nanny. She used to like *Me He Manurere* so I played it for her, and I could hear her quavering voice singing in her room.

Me he manurere aue . . .

When I finally left Nanny I told her I would come back in the morning.

But that night, Nanny Tama rang up.

'Your Nanny Miro, she's dying.'

We all rushed to Nanny's house. It was already crowded. All the old women were there. Nanny was lying very still. Then she looked up and whispered to Mrs Heta:

'Maka . . . Maka tiko bum . . . I want a game of cards . . .'

A pack of cards was found. The old ladies sat around the bed, playing. Everybody else decided to play cards too, to keep Nanny company. The men played poker in the kitchen and sitting room. The kids played snap in the other bedrooms. The house overflowed with card players, even onto the lawn outside Nanny's window, where she could see . . .

The women laid the cards out on the bed. They dealt the first hand. They cackled and joked with Nanny, trying not to cry. And Mrs Heta kept saying to Nanny:

'Eee! You cheat Miro. You cheat!' And she made her googly eye reach far over to see Nanny's cards.

'You think you can see, ay, Maka tiko bum?' Nanny

---

1. *lav* : (informal) abbreviation of lavatory.

coughed. You think you're going to win this hand, ay? Well, take that!

She slammed down a full house.

The other women goggled at the cards. Mrs Heta looked at her own cards. Then she smiled through her tears and yelled:

'Eee! You cheat Miro! I got two aces in my hand already! Only four in the pack. So how come you got three aces in your hand?'

Everybody laughed. Nanny and Mrs Heta started squabbling as they always did, pointing at each other and saying: You the cheat, not me! And Nanny Miro said: 'I saw you, Maka tiko bum, I saw you sneaking that card from under the blanket.'

She began to laugh. Quietly. Her eyes streaming with tears.

And while she was laughing, she died.

Everybody was silent. Then Mrs Heta took the cards from Nanny's hands and kissed her.

'You the cheat, Miro, she whispered. You the cheat yourself . . .'

We buried Nanny on the hill with the rest of her family. During her tangi, [1] Mrs Heta played patience with Nanny, spreading the cards across the casket. [2]

Later in the year, Mrs Heta, she died too. She was buried right next to Nanny, so that they could keep on playing cards . . .

And I bet you they're still squabbling up there . . .

'Eee! You cheat Miro . . .'

'You the cheat, Maka tiko bum. You, you the cheat . . .'

---

1. *tangi* : (Maori) funeral.
2. *casket* : coffin.

Characters

1. Nanny Miro is represented as full of contradictions. Complete the sentences below to show this.

    i. She has a lot of money, but . . .
    ii. She gets impatient with children, yet . . .
    iii. She constantly accuses Mrs Heta of cheating; nevertheless, . . .

    Is this convincing characterisation?

2. The story gives us a strong sense of an enclosed Maori community. In what ways does this community seem to differ from the rest of New Zealand society? Is the narrator fully committed to the Maori community?

Setting

1. Where does most of the action of this story take place? How does this setting change in the course of the story?

2. Are there more than three rooms in Nanny Miro's house, or fewer than three?

Structure

1. What grammatical form does the writer use to distinguish between the 'now' of the story and the narrator's memories of Nanny Miro?

2. What is the effect of the first paragraph of the story? Why has the author chosen to open the story in this way?

3. Re-read the account of Nanny Miro's last game of cards. How does it illustrate the community's affection for the old woman?

Language

1. Much of the dialogue is grammatically unconventional. What irregularities do you notice? What does this suggest about the Maoris?

2. Attempt a definition of the following expressions, using the context to help you:

   i. mokopuna
   ii. hoha kids
   iii. Maka tiko bum
   iv. Haere mai
   v. teka

   Would the story be more or less effective without these Maori expressions?

3. It seems that 'You the cheat' has a special meaning when Mrs Heta says it to Nanny Miro immediately after her death. How would you interpret it at that point?

Narrator

1. The first-person narrator may be an observer or an active participant in the story. Which is the case here?

2. Could the story have been narrated by Mrs Heta? In what way(s) would its effect have been changed?

Themes

1. Does the community here remind you of the community in another story you have read in this volume? Which? What do they have in common?

2. Is it natural for different ethnic groups to form separate communities within the same country? Is it desirable?

West Indies

Bogart

V. S. Naipaul

V. S. Naipaul (Vididhar Surajprasad Naipaul) 1932-

Educated in Trinidad and at the University of Oxford, Naipaul has lived in England since 1950, although he often spends long periods abroad. This has inevitably led to his being a somewhat ambivalent figure: 'English' to his fellow West Indians, 'foreign' to the English among whom he lives. He has set many of his novels and stories in Trinidad, such as *A House for Mr Biswas,* his first major novel, published in 1961: Mr Biswas, based on the author's father, is a Trinidadian of Indian origins, and many of his other protagonists are West Indians. In addition to his novels and short stories, he has written a number of political books which are deeply pessimistic. *Bogart* is typical of his earlier style, in which he used comedy to sweeten his criticism of West Indian society.

EVERY MORNING WHEN HE GOT UP Hat would sit on the banister of his back verandah and shout across, 'What happening there, Bogart?'

Bogart would turn in his bed and mumble softly, so that no one heard, 'What happening there, Hat?'

It was something of a mystery why he was called Bogart; but I suspect that it was Hat who gave him the name. I don't know if you remember the year the film *Casablanca* was made. That was the year when Bogart's fame spread like fire through Port of Spain and hundreds of young men began adopting the hard-boiled [1] Bogartian attitude.

Before they called him Bogart they called him Patience, [2] because he played that game from morn till night. Yet he never liked cards.

Whenever you went over to Bogart's little room you found him sitting on his bed with the cards in seven lines on a small table in front of him.

'What happening there, man?' he would ask quietly, and then he would say nothing for ten or fifteen minutes. And somehow you felt you couldn't really talk to Bogart, he looked so bored and superior. His eyes were small and sleepy. His face

---

1. *hard-boiled* : unemotional, not showing feelings.
2. *Patience* : a card game for one player, sometimes called 'Solitaire'.

was fat and his hair was gleaming black. His arms were plump. Yet he was not a funny man. He did everything with a captivating languor. Even when he licked his thumb to deal out the cards there was grace in it.

He was the most bored man I ever knew.

He made a pretence of making a living by tailoring, and he had even paid me some money to write a sign for him:

TAILOR AND CUTTER [1]
Suits made to Order
Popular and Competitive Prices

He bought a sewing-machine and some blue and white and brown chalks. But I never could imagine him competing with anyone; and I cannot remember him making a suit. He was a little bit like Popo, the carpenter next door, who never made a stick of furniture, and was always planing and chiselling and making what I think he called mortises. [2] Whenever I asked him, 'Mr Popo, what you making?' he would reply, 'Ha, boy! That's the question. I making the thing without a name.' Bogart was never even making anything like this.

Being a child, I never wondered how Bogart came by any money. I assumed that grown-ups had money as a matter of course. Popo had a wife who worked at a variety of jobs; and ended up by becoming the friend of many men. I could never think of Bogart as having mother or father; and he never brought a woman to his little room. This little room of his was called the servant-room but no servant to the people in the main house ever lived there. It was just an architectural convention.

It is still something of a miracle to me that Bogart managed to make friends. Yet he did make many friends; he was at one

---

1. *cutter* : a person whose job is cutting cloth to make clothes.
2. *mortise* ['mɔːtɪs] : a hole cut in a piece of wood to take another piece, called the tenon, thus forming a joint.

time quite the most popular man in the street. I used to see him squatting on the pavement with all the big men of the street. And while Hat or Edward or Eddoes was talking, Bogart would just look down and draw rings with his fingers on the pavement. He never laughed audibly. He never told a story. Yet whenever there was a fête [1] or something like that, everybody would say, 'We must have Bogart. He smart like hell, [2] that man.' In a way he gave them great solace and comfort, I suppose.

And so every morning, as I told you, Hat would shout, very loudly, 'What happening there, Bogart?'

And he would wait for the indeterminate grumble which was Bogart saying, 'What happening there, Hat?'

But one morning, when Hat shouted, there was no reply. Something which had appeared unalterable was missing.

Bogart had vanished; had left us without a word.

The men in the street were silent and sorrowful for two whole days. They assembled in Bogart's little room. Hat lifted up the deck of cards that lay on Bogart's table and dropped two or three cards at a time reflectively.

Hat said, 'You think he gone Venezuela?'

But no one knew. Bogart told them so little.

And the next morning Hat got up and lit a cigarette and went to his back verandah and was on the point of shouting, when he remembered. He milked the cows earlier than usual that morning, and the cows didn't like it.

A month passed; then another month. Bogart didn't return.

Hat and his friends began using Bogart's room as their clubhouse. They played *wappee* and drank rum and smoked, and sometimes brought the odd stray woman [3] to the room. Hat was

---

1. *fête* [feɪt] : (French) a day of public entertainment, usually held outdoors, often to collect money for charitable causes.

2. *smart like hell* : (informal) very clever.

3. *odd stray woman* : occasional woman they had met by chance.

presently involved with the police for gambling and sponsoring cock-fighting; and he had to spend a lot of money to bribe his way out of trouble.

It was as if Bogart had never come to Miguel Street. And after all Bogart had been living in the street only for four years or so. He had come one day with a single suitcase, looking for a room, and he had spoken to Hat who was squatting outside his gate, smoking a cigarette and reading the cricket scores in the evening paper. Even then he hadn't said much. All he said – that was Hat's story – was, 'You know any rooms?' and Hat had led him to the next yard where there was this furnished servant-room going for eight dollars a month. He had installed himself there immediately, brought out a pack of cards, and begun playing patience.

This impressed Hat.

For the rest he had always remained a man of mystery. He became Patience.

When Hat and everybody else had forgotten or nearly forgotten Bogart, he returned. He turned up one morning just about seven and found Eddoes had a woman on his bed. The woman jumped up and screamed. Eddoes jumped up, not so much afraid as embarrassed.

Bogart said, 'Move over. I tired and I want to sleep.'

He slept until five that afternoon, and when he woke up he found his room full of the old gang. Eddoes was being very loud and noisy to cover up his embarrassment. Hat had brought a bottle of rum.

Hat said, 'What happening there, Bogart?'

And he rejoiced when he found his cue taken up. [1] 'What happening there, Hat?'

Hat opened the bottle of rum, and shouted to Boyee to go buy a bottle of soda water.

---

1. *his cue taken up* : his signal for Bogart to speak followed in the expected way. In the theatre, a cue is the signal for an actor to do or say something specific.

Bogart asked, 'How the cows, Hat?'

'They all right.'

'And Boyee?'

'He all right too. Ain't you just hear me call him?'

'And Errol?'

'He all right too. But what happening, Bogart? You all right?'

Bogart nodded, and drank a long Madrassi [1] shot [2] of rum. Then another, and another; and they had presently finished the bottle.

'Don't worry.' Bogart said. 'I go buy another.'

They had never seen Bogart drink so much; they had never heard him talk so much; and they were alarmed. No one dared to ask Bogart where he had been.

Bogart said, 'You boys been keeping my room hot all the time.'

'It wasn't the same without you,' Hat replied.

But they were all worried. Bogart was hardly opening his lips when he spoke. His mouth was twisted a little, and his accent was getting slightly American.

'Sure, sure,' Bogart said, and he had got it right. He was just like an actor.

Hat wasn't sure that Bogart was drunk.

In appearance, you must know, Hat recalled Rex Harrison, [3] and he had done his best to strengthen the resemblance. He combed his hair backwards) screwed up [4] his eyes, and he spoke very nearly like Harrison.

'Damn it, Bogart,' Hat said, and he became very like Rex Harrison. 'You may as well tell us everything right away.'

---

1. *Madrassi* : imported from Madras in India.
2. *shot* : alcoholic drink, usually small.
3. *Rex Harrison* : British actor (1908-90), known for his elegant appearance and refined accent.
4. *screwed up* : made narrower.

Bogart showed his teeth and laughed in a twisted, cynical way.

'Sure I'll tell,' he said, and got up and stuck his thumbs inside his waistband. 'Sure, I'll tell everything.'

He lit a cigarette, leaned back in such a way that the smoke got into his eyes; and, squinting, he drawled out [1] his story.

He had got a job on a ship and had gone to British Guiana. There he had deserted, and gone into the interior. He became a cowboy on the Rupununi, [2] smuggled things (he didn't say what) into Brazil, and had gathered some girls from Brazil and taken them to Georgetown. He was running the best brothel in the town when the police treacherously took his bribes and arrested him.

'It was a high-class place,' he said, 'no bums. [3] Judges and doctors and big shot [4] civil servants.'

'What happen?' Eddoes asked. 'Jail?'

'How you so stupid?' Hat said. 'Jail, when the man here with we. But why you people so stupid? Why you don t let the man talk?'

But Bogart was offended, and refused to speak another word.

From then on the relationship between these men changed. Bogart became the Bogart of the films. Hat became Harrison. And the morning exchange became this:

'Bogart!'

'Shaddup, [5] Hat!'

---

1. *drawled out* : told slowly, with exaggeratedly long vowels.
2. *Rupununi* : a river in British Guiana, South America.
3. *bums* : worthless people.
4. *big shot* : (here used as an adjective) important.
5. *shaddup* : approximately phonetic spelling to show Bogart's pronunciation of 'Shut up'.

Bogart now became the most feared man in the street. Even Big Foot was said to be afraid of him. Bogart drank and swore and gambled with the best. He shouted rude remarks at girls walking by themselves in the street. He bought a hat, and pulled down the brim over his eyes. He became a regular sight, standing against the high concrete fence of his yard, hands in his pockets, one foot jammed against the wall, and an eternal cigarette in his mouth.

Then he disappeared again. He was playing cards with the gang in his room, and he got up and said, 'I'm going to the latrine.'

They didn't see him for four months.

When he returned, he had grown a little fatter but he had become a little more aggressive. His accent was now pure American. To complete the imitation, he began being expansive towards children. He called out to them in the streets, and gave them money to buy gum and chocolate. He loved stroking their heads, and giving them good advice.

The third time he went away and came back he gave a great party in his room for all the children or kids, as he called them. He bought cases of Solo [1] and Coca-Cola and Pepsi-Cola and about a bushel [2] of cakes.

Then Sergeant Charles, the policeman who lived up Miguel Street at number forty-five, came and arrested Bogart.

'Don't act tough, [3] Bogart,' Sergeant Charles said.

But Bogart failed to take the cue.

'What happening, man? I ain't do anything.'

Sergeant Charles told him.

There was a little stir [4] in the papers. The charge was bigamy; but it was up to Hat to find out all the inside details that the newspapers never mention.

---

1. *Solo* : a non-alcoholic drink.
2. *bushel* ['buʃəl] : a measure of capacity.
3. *act tough* [tʌf] : behave as if you were very strong.
4. *stir* : excitement.

'You see,' Hat said on the pavement that evening, 'the man leave his first wife in Tunapuna and come to Port of Spain. They couldn't have children. He remain here feeling sad and small. He go away, find a girl in Caroni and he give she a baby. In Caroni they don't make joke about that sort of thing and Bogart had to get married to the girl.'

'But why he leave she?' Eddoes asked.

'To be a man, among we men.'

Characters

1. If you have not seen *Casablanca*, find out what kind of character was played in the film by Humphrey Bogart, after which you can decide whether 'Bogart' is an appropriate nickname for the character in this story.

2. How would you define Hat's relationship with Bogart?

Setting

1. What social class do the people in the story belong to? Support your answer with quotations from the text.

2. Apart from Bogart's room, where do the characters in this story spend most of their time?

Structure

1. Are the events in the story narrated in chronological order?

2. Bogart's absences are reported increasingly briefly. Note down how many lines are devoted to each absence. Why, in your opinion, has Naipaul structured the story in this way?

3. There are a number of very short paragraphs, consisting of a single sentence, in this story. Underline them and suggest a reason for this feature.

Symbolism

Is Bogart's card-playing symbolic? If so, what does it symbolise?

Language

1. The dialogue in *Bogart* does not follow standard grammatical structures. What irregularities can you identify? Have you found anything similar in other stories in this book?

2. What do you think *wappee* is?

    i.   a card game;
    ii. a ball game;
    iii. a kind of music.

Narrator

Who is the narrator? Look for information about her/him in the text. How does the choice of this particular narrator affect the story?

Themes

Bogart seems to change his appearance and personality at will. What do you feel about the stability (or instability) of human personality? Why is Bogart so much admired in his community?

I Used To Live Here Once

JEAN RHYS

Jean Rhys 1894-1979

Ella Gwendolen Rees Williams came to England from the West Indian island of Dominica in her teens and worked for some years as a chorus girl; in 1919 she went to Paris, where she wrote her early novels, all to some degree autobiographical. She was thought to have died, but was rediscovered living in South-West England in 1958 and made an astonishing return to the literary world with her most famous novel, *Wide Sargasso Sea* (1966), which tells the story of the first wife of Mr Rochester, the male protagonist of Charlotte Brontë's *Jane Eyre*. She then published two volumes of short stories which confirmed her already high reputation. In the last twenty years of her life she won many honours and awards. Rhys's stories often deal with madness, which she herself had experienced.

SHE WAS STANDING BY the river looking at the stepping stones and remembering each one. There was the round unsteady stone, the pointed one, the flat one in the middle – the safe stone where you could stand and look round. The next wasn't so safe for when the river was full the water flowed over it and even when it showed dry it was slippery. But after that it was easy and soon she was standing on the other side.

The road was much wider than it used to be but the work had been done carelessly. The felled [1] trees had not been cleared away and the bushes looked trampled. Yet it was the same road and she walked along feeling extraordinarily happy.

It was a fine day, a blue day. The only thing was that the sky had a glassy look that she didn't remember. That was the only word she could think of. Glassy. She turned the corner, saw that what had been the old pavé [2] had been taken up, and there too the road was much wider, but it had the same unfinished look.

She came to the worn stone steps that led up to the house and her heart began to beat. The screw pine [3] was gone, so was

---

1. *felled* : cut down (of trees).
2. *pavé* : (French) paved road or path.
3. *screw-pine* : a kind of tree found in the West Indies and in other tropical countries.

the mock [1] summer house called the ajoupa, but the clove tree [2] was still there and at the top of the steps the rough lawn stretched away, just as she remembered it. She stopped and looked towards the house that had been added to and painted white. It was strange to see a car standing in front of it.

There were two children under the big mango tree, a boy and a little girl, and she waved to them and called 'Hello' but they didn't answer her or turn their heads. Very fair children, as Europeans born in the West Indies so often are: as if the white blood is asserting itself against all odds.

The grass was yellow in the hot sunlight as she walked towards them. When she was quite close she called again, shyly: 'Hello.' Then, 'I used to live here once,' she said.

Still they didn't answer. When she said for the third time 'Hello' she was quite near them. Her arms went out instinctively with the longing to touch them.

It was the boy who turned. His grey eyes looked straight into hers. His expression didn't change. He said: 'Hasn't it gone cold all of a sudden. D'you notice? Let's go in.' 'Yes let's,' said the girl.

Her arms fell to her sides as she watched them running across the grass to the house. That was the first time she knew.

1. *mock* : (here) imitation.
2. *clove tree* : a kind of tree found in the West Indies; the dried flowers of this tree are used as a spice.

Characters

What do we learn about the protagonist of this story? How old do you think she is? Why do the children refuse to speak to her?

Setting

At what point in the story do we discover where it takes place? Are there any indications before this point to show that it is not in Europe?

Symbolism

Re-read the opening paragraph. In the light of the ending of the story, what might the river and the stepping-stones symbolise?

Narrator

This story is told from the point of view of:

  i.   an omniscient narrator;
 ii.   the protagonist;
iii.   mostly the protagonist, with some exceptions.

Justify your answer by detailed reference to the text.

Themes

Write a short essay on the dangers of nostalgia.

Post-reading Activities

Questions about the Whole Volume

Characters

1. In which stories is the main character male and in which is the main character female? Complete the chart below.

MALE	FEMALE

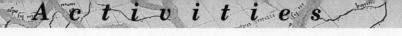

2. The first-person narrator is not necessarily the most important character in the story s/he tells. Who is the most important character in each of the eight first-person narratives you have read here?

TITLE	THE MOST IMPORTANT CHARACTER
The Union Buries Its Dead	
The Persimonn Tree	
The Summer My Grandmother Was Supposed To Die	
When Sikh Meets Sikh	
The Hole That Jack Dug	
A Game Of Cards	
Bogart	

Did you find it particularly difficult to decide which is the main character in some of these stories? Which ones? Why?

3. In which story or stories is there evidence of tension or conflict between people of different racial origins?

Setting

1. These stories represent post-colonial literature: that is, they were written by citizens of countries which, until quite recently, were colonies of Great Britain, and which have continued to use the language of their colonisers for many official and literary purposes.

   Which stories seem to reflect a culture which is strikingly non-European? What particular differences have you noticed in this respect?

2. Which stories emphasise material poverty?

3. Why are the physical surroundings so important in *A Horse And Two Goats*? Why are they less important in *The Hole That Jack Dug*?

Structure

1. The stories in this volume are structured in various ways.

   i. Arrange the stories in descending order of length (i.e. from the longest to the shortest).

   ii. Note which stories are divided into sections (indicated by a blank line between two blocks of text).

2. Any narrative includes some or all of the following elements:

   - dialogue
   - description (of people or places)
   - incident
   - comment (by the author or one of the characters).

   Are all these elements present in all the stories in this volume?

Symbolism

1. Discuss the following symbols:

    i. shoes and feet in *The Only American From Our Village*
    ii. music in *The Bridegroom*

    Which do you find most effective?

2. Look again at the titles of the stories in this volume. Which of them are symbolic and which are merely factual or descriptive? Are you more stimulated by the first or by the second of these kinds of titles?

Language

1. How many languages, apart from English, are used in these stories? List them together with the titles of the stories in which they are found.

2. Find at least three examples of figurative language (simile, metaphor or personification) in each of the following stories:

When Sikh Meets Sikh	
The Only American From Our Village	
A Horse And Two Goats	

What do they add to the effect of the story?

Narrator

1. Three of the stories in this volume are told from a child's point of view. Which are they? Is the effect the same in all three cases?

2. Find three examples of intrusion by the narrator in a third-person narrative. Do you find them disturbing, or do they help you to understand the story?

Themes

1. In some of these stories, an ethnic minority is shown preserving its traditions. Is complete integration possible? Is it desirable? Give your reasons.

2. Which of the four Continents represented here seems most attractive to you? Has your view of any of the Continents changed as a result of reading these stories? Explain your answers.

3. Compare the attitude to women in *Minutes Of Glory* and in *The Bridegroom*.

4. Compare the view of the USA suggested in *The Only American From Our Village* and in *A Horse And Two Goats*.

5. What is the role of religion in *The Union Buries Its Dead*, in *A Sacrificial Egg* and in *The Summer My Grandmother Was Supposed To Die*?

6. Write an essay on the relationship between different generations in *Good Advice Is Better Than Rubies* and *A Game Of Cards*.

7. Which of these stories could be most easily adapted for television? Are there any which could not be adapted for that medium? Give reasons for your answers.

8. Which story or stories did you find most effective? Why? Before you began reading, you looked at the titles of all the stories and decided which were the most interesting. Were your expectations fulfilled?

9. In which of the cultures represented here would you find it most difficult to feel at ease? Analyse the characteristics of their various ways of life. What factors would create difficulties for you if you found yourself living in one of these communities?

10. Is it possible to identify certain attitudes or situations as universal, or are they invariably conditioned by the surrounding culture?